И.А. Шишкова
М.Е. Вербовская

Давай говорить по-английски!

Учебник английского языка для начальной школы

Под редакцией Н.А. Бонк

ПЕРВЫЙ ГОД ОБУЧЕНИЯ

МОСКВА
ОНИКС
1999

ББК 46.2
Ш 65

Авторы выражают глубокую признательность и благодарность за неоценимую помощь в подготовке этой книги Наталье Александровне Бонк и Ирине Анатольевне Бонк, а также преподавателям Дублинского университета Саре Смит и Кей Доноху за стилистическое редактирование английского текстового материала.

И.А. Шишкова, М.Е. Вербовская

Художники
М.И. Истомин, И.В. Попов

Дизайн обложки С.А. Салтанова

Макет К.И. Заботиной

Шишкова И.А., Вербовская М.Е.

Ш 65 Давай говорить по-английски! / Под редакцией Н.А. Бонк. Учебн. — М.: Издательский Дом ОНИКС, 1999. — 192 с., ил.

ISBN 5-249-00132-7

Свой новый учебник «Давай говорить по-английски!» и рабочую тетрадь с тем же названием авторы адресуют детям 6—9 лет, которые начинают изучать английский язык в 1—2 классах школы или дома с родителями.

Художественный редактор А.М. Титова
Технический редактор К.И. Заботина
Корректор З.Ф. Юрескул
Компьютерная вёрстка С.В. Пильта

ЛР №065803 от 9.04.98 г.
Подписано в печать с готовых диапозитивов 30.11.99.
Формат 60х90 $^1/_8$. Печать офсетная. Усл. печ. л. 24,0.
Доп. тираж 15 000 экз. Заказ 3654.

ЗАО «Издательский Дом ОНИКС»
107066, Москва, ул. Доброслободская, 5а
Отдел реализации: тел. (095) 310-75-25, 255-51-02

При участии ООО «Фирма «Издательство АСТ»
ЛР № 066236 от 22.12.98 г.
366720, РФ, Республика Ингушетия,
г.Назрань, ул.Московская, 13а
Наши электронные адреса:
WWW.AST.RU E-mail: astpub@aha.ru

АООТ «Тверской полиграфический комбинат»
170024, г. Тверь, пр-т Ленина, 5.

© И.А. Шишкова, М.Е. Вербовская, 1998
© М.И. Истомин, И.В. Попов, иллюстрации, 1998

ISBN 5-249-00132-7   © ЗАО «Издательский Дом ОНИКС», макет, оформление, 1998

1 A cat. A bat

ЗАПОМНИ НАЗВАНИЯ БУКВ

Aa [eɪ]   **Pp** [piː]

Bb [biː]   **Tt** [tiː]

Cc [siː]   **Gg** [dʒiː]

НОВЫЕ СЛОВА

a cat [kæt]   кошка

a cap [kæp]   кепка

a bat [bæt]   летучая мышь

a bag [bæg]   сумка

a cat

a cap

a bat

a bag

1. Назови буквы.

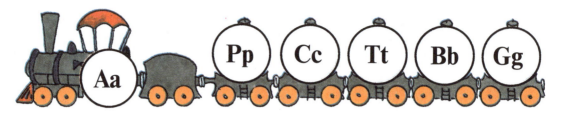

2. Соедини одинаковые маленькие и большие буквы.

БУКВЫ И ЗВУКИ

Некоторые буквы передают только один звук. Посмотри на слово **bat**. Первая буква **b** передаёт звук [b].

Последняя буква **t** передаёт звук [t].

А теперь взгляни на слово **cap**. Последняя буква **p** передаёт в нем звук [p].

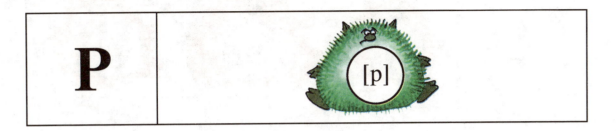

Есть буквы, которые могут передавать несколько звуков. Например, буква **c** в уже известном тебе слове **cap** читается [k], но может читаться [s] в других словах.

Буква **Gg** читается [g] и [dʒ].

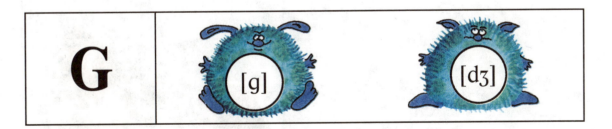

Слово **bag** оканчивается на букву **g**, которая читается [g].

О звуках [s] и [dʒ] мы поговорим в другом уроке.

Буква **Aa** передаёт целых три звука!

Сейчас мы пока познакомимся с двумя звуками этой буквы [ə] и [æ]. Они хотят с тобой поздороваться. Посмотри, какой сильный звук [æ] и какой слабый звук [ə]. Вообще-то он очень хороший, но его надо произносить тихонько, без усилий.

Приведём такой пример: **a cat**. Маленькое слово **a** читается [ə] и показывает, что мы говорим о какой-нибудь одной кошке. Буква **a** в слове **cat** читается [æ]. А теперь посмотри на слова и скажи, где буква **a** читается [ə], а где [æ].

a cat

a bat

a cap

a bag

Третий звук [eɪ] буквы **Aa** тоже сильный, но о нём мы поговорим в другом уроке.

3. Соедини линией буквы с их звуками. Вот так:

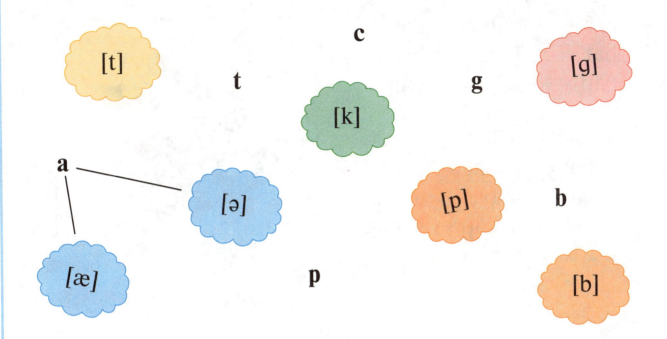

4. Соедини линией слова с картинками.

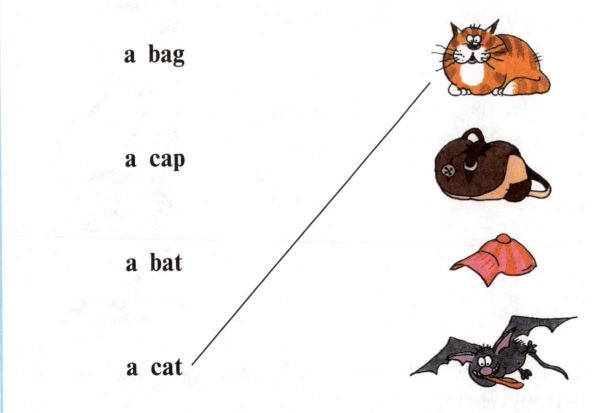

5. Прочитай.

cat cat cat
bat bat bat
cap cap cap

a cat a bat a cap
a bat a cat a bag
a cap a bag a bat
a cat a cap a bag

6. Прочитай слова. Подбери слово к картинке и обведи его кружком. Вот так:

a cat, a bat, a bag, (a cap)

a bat, a bag, a cap, a cat

a cap, a bag, a cat, a bat

a cat, a bag, a cap, a bat

Сколько раз тебе встретилось слово **cat**? Найди его, покажи и прочитай.

2 Make a cake, Kate!

Kate

a plate

ЗАПОМНИ НАЗВАНИЯ БУКВ

Nn [en]

Kk [keɪ]

Ll [el]

Mm [em]

Jj [dʒeɪ]

Ee [i:]

Jane

a cake

НОВЫЕ СЛОВА

Kate	[keɪt]	имя девочки
Jane	[dʒeɪn]	имя девочки
a plate	[pleɪt]	тарелка
a cake	[keɪk]	пирожное, торт
take	[teɪk]	брать, взять
make	[meɪk]	делать, сделать

1. Назови буквы.

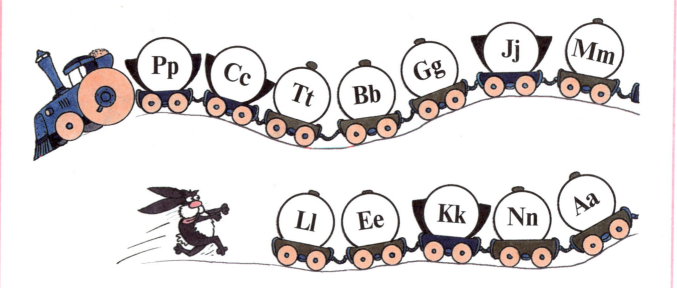

2. Соедини одинаковые маленькие и большие буквы.

БУКВЫ И ЗВУКИ

Ты уже знаешь, что некоторые буквы могут передавать только один звук, например, буквы **Nn**, **Ll**, **Mm** и **Kk**.

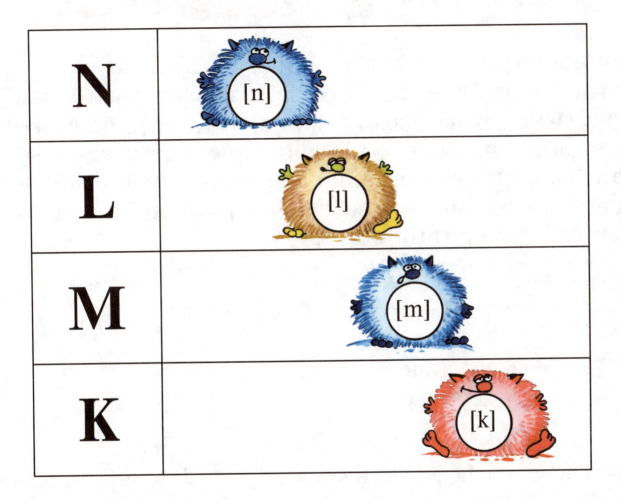

Ты помнишь, что буква **Aa** читается [ə] и [æ]? Например, [ə'kæt]. Теперь третий звук этой буквы [eɪ] хочет с тобой познакомиться.

11

Посмотри!

Он немножко заважничал, потому что его зовут так же, как и букву **Aa** – [eɪ]. Этот звук живёт в таких словах, как **make** [meɪk], **take** [teɪk], **plate** [pleɪt], **cake** [keɪk], и многих других. Обрати внимание, что в конце всех этих слов стоит буква **e**, но она не читается, она немая. Для чего же она нужна? А для того чтобы показать, как следует прочитать букву **Aa**.

Сравни:

[eɪ]	[æ]
Kate	cat
cake	cap

Имя девочки Jane начинается с буквы **Jj** [dʒeɪ]. Запомни, что эта буква – хозяйка звука [dʒ]. Видишь, он хочет с тобой познакомиться и машет тебе флажком.

Последняя буква **e** в слове **Jane**, как ты уже знаешь, пишется, но не читается.

3. Соедини линией буквы с их звуками.

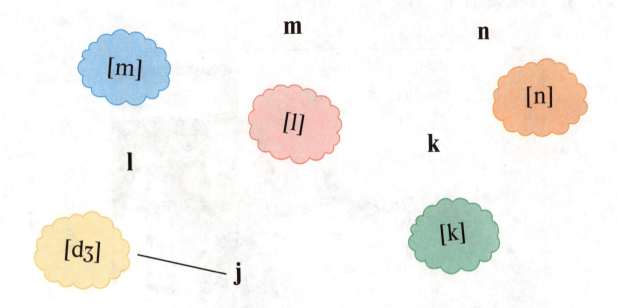

4. Соедини линией слова с картинками.

5. Прочитай каждое слово по два раза.

Kate Kate   plate plate   take take
Jane Jane   cake cake   make make

ЗАПОМНИ, как можно попросить кого-нибудь что-то сделать. Посмотри на картинки.

Мама говорит: «Кейт, возьми пирожное.»

А бабушка просит Джейн испечь торт.

6. Прочитай и переведи.

Kate, take a cake. Jane, take a cake. Jane, take a plate. Kate, take a plate. Jane, make a cake. Kate, make a cake.

Сколько раз тебе встретилось слово **cake**? Найди его, покажи и прочитай.

7. Прочитай слова. Подбери слово к картинке и обведи его кружком. Вот так:

Jane, (Kate,) a plate, a cake

a plate, Jane, Kate, a cake

Kate, a cake, a plate, Jane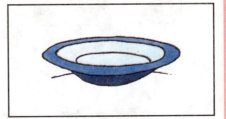

a cake, Jane, Kate, a plate

8. Помоги Джейн и Кейт добраться до магазина, в котором продаётся вкусный торт. Скажи, кто им встретился по дороге.

3 A lamp and a table

ЗАПОМНИ НАЗВАНИЯ БУКВ

Rr [ɑ:]
Ff [ef]
Hh [eɪtʃ]
Dd [di:]

a rat

a table

НОВЫЕ СЛОВА

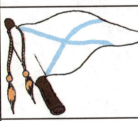
a flag

a rat	[ræt]	крыса
a flag	[flæg]	флаг
a hat	[hæt]	шляпа
a table	['teɪbl]	стол
a lake	[leɪk]	озеро
a mat	[mæt]	коврик
a lamp	[læmp]	лампа
bad	[bæd]	плохой
fat	[fæt]	толстый

a lake

a hat

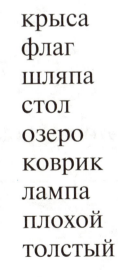

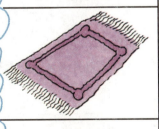
a mat

a lamp

1. Назови буквы.

2. Соедини одинаковые маленькие и большие буквы.

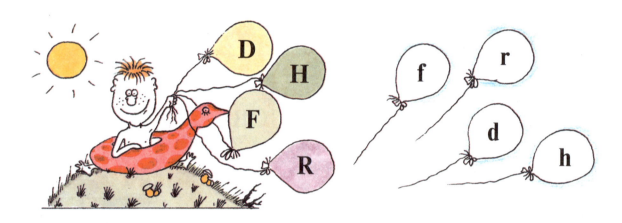

БУКВЫ И ЗВУКИ

Каждая буква этого урока передаёт только один звук.

Так, в слове **rat** первая буква **r** передаёт звук [r].

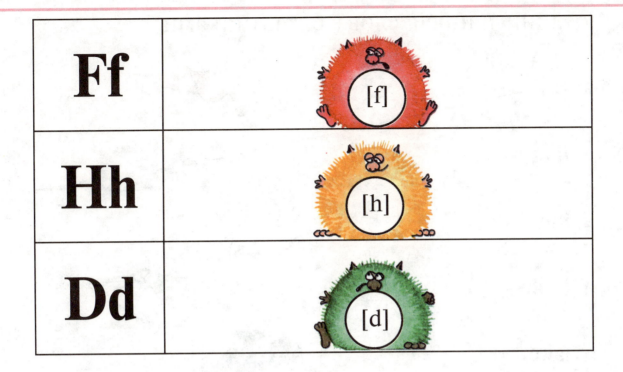

В слове **fat** первая буква **f** передаёт звук [f]. В слове **hat** первая буква **h** читается [h], а последняя буква **d** в слове **bad** читается [d].

3. Соедини линией буквы с их звуками.

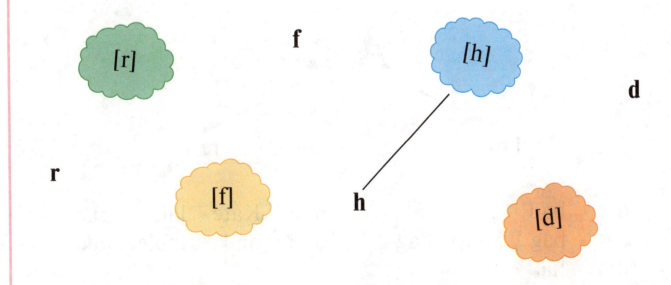

4. Соедини линией слова с картинками.

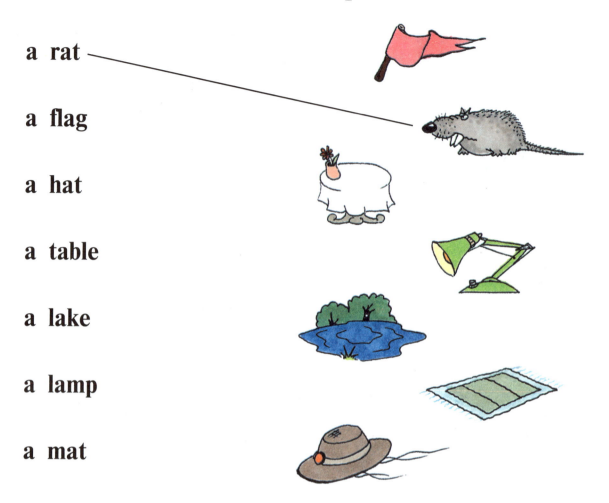

- **a rat**
- **a flag**
- **a hat**
- **a table**
- **a lake**
- **a lamp**
- **a mat**

5. Прочитай слова со звуками [æ] и [eɪ].

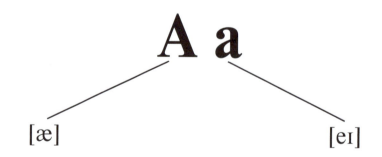

[æ]				[eɪ]			
cat	bad	fat	rat	Jane	Kate	lake	plate
bat	bag	lamp	flag	cake	make	table	take
mat	hat						

ЗАПОМНИ слово **and** [ænd] — **и**. Оно почти никогда не произносится с ударением. Поэтому вместо звука [æ] читается [ə] — [ənd].

6. Послушай внимательно, как произносится слово **and**, и прочитай вместе с преподавателем. Переведи фразы.

bad and fat
a cat and a rat
a bad fat cat and a bad fat rat

a lamp and a flag
a bad lamp and a bad flag
a plate and a cake

Kate and Jane
Make a cake, Kate.
Jane, take a plate.
Jane, take a cake and a plate.
Take a plate and a cake, Kate.

Сколько раз тебе встретилось слово **plate**? Найди его, покажи и прочитай.

7. Прочитай.

   a rat and a cat
   a rat, a cat and a lamp
   a rat, a cat, a lamp and a hat
   a rat, a cat, a lamp, a hat and a flag
   a rat, a cat, a lamp, a hat, a flag and a bag
   a rat, a cat, a lamp, a hat, a flag, a bag and a mat

8. Соедини линией слова, которые рифмуются. Вот так:

a cat

a plate   a mat   a bag

             a bat

         Kate

a rat   a hat

   take   a flag

  a cake   make

4 Hi, Mike!

ЗАПОМНИ НАЗВАНИЯ БУКВ

Ii [aɪ]
Vv [vi:]

Выучи новые слова. В них буква Ii читается так, как она называется в алфавите [aɪ]. Буква v в слове **five** читается [v].

I [aɪ] — я

a bike [baɪk] — велосипед

ride [raɪd] — ездить

five [faɪv] — пять

nine [naɪn] — девять

a kite [kaɪt] — воздушный змей

Mike [maɪk] — имя мальчика

I

5
five

a kite

a bike

9
nine

Mike

1. Прочитай каждое слово по два раза.

I I five five nine nine Mike Mike
bike bike kite kite ride ride

БУКВЫ И ЗВУКИ

ЗАПОМНИ название буквы **Ss** [es]. Буква **Ss** очень важна, потому что она помогает поставить слово во **множественное число**.

Если у тебя одна кошка, ты скажешь **a cat**. Это называется **единственное число**, потому что кошка одна, а если у тебя две или больше кошек, ты скажешь **cats**. Это называется **множественное число**, потому что кошек много. Посмотри, во множественном числе к слову **cat** прибавилась буква **s**, а маленькое слово **a** убежало.

Буква **Ss** во множественном числе читается [s] или [z]. Например:

	[s]		[z]
a cat	cat**s**	a bag	bag**s**
a cap	cap**s**	a flag	flag**s**
a kite	kite**s**	a table	table**s**

2. Прочитай и переведи.

a cat, five cats, nine cats   a cap, five caps, nine caps
a bag, five bags, nine bags   a bike, five bikes, nine bikes
a kite, five kites, nine kites   a cake, five cakes, nine cakes

Mike, ride a bike. Mike, make a kite.

Теперь, зная букву **Ii**, ты сможешь поздороваться с друзьями вот так: **Hi** [haɪ]! **Привет**!

Если тебе кто-то или что-то нравится, ты можешь сказать:

I like Mike. Мне нравится Майк.
I like bikes. Мне нравятся велосипеды.

ЗАПОМНИ:

like [laɪk] — нравиться, любить

3. Прочитай и переведи.

Hi, Mike! Hi, Jane! Hi, Kate!

I like Mike. I like Jane. I like Kate.
I like bikes. I like kites. I like bags. I like flags.

Five fat cats. Nine fat cats. I like fat cats.
Nine bats. I like bats.

Five cakes. Nine cakes. I like cakes.

Hi, Mike! Mike, take a bike.
Ride a bike, Mike.
Mike, take a kite and a bike.

Jane, take five cakes. Take five plates, Jane.
Kate, make nine cakes. Take nine plates, Kate.

4. Соедини линией буквы с их звуками. Вот так:

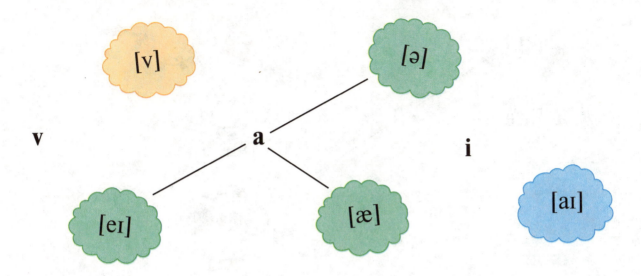

5. Прочитай слова. Подбери слово к картинке и обведи его кружком.

a bike, a bag, Kate, (a kite)

a kite, Mike, Kate, a bike

five, nine, Mike, a kite

6. Соедини линией слова с картинками. Вот так:

a bike

a kite

five

nine

7. Подбери подписи к картинкам. Соедини их линиями. Вот так:

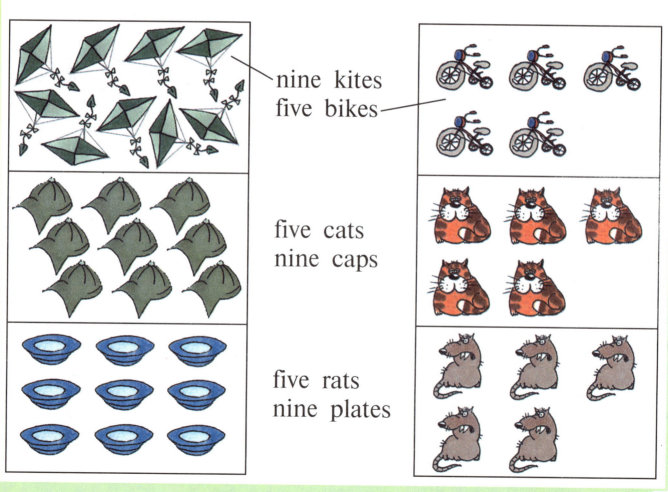

nine kites
five bikes

five cats
nine caps

five rats
nine plates

5 It's a cat

Ты уже знаешь много слов, в которых буква **Ii** читается [aɪ].
Например: **Mike**, **bike**, **kite**, **five**, **nine**.

А теперь выучи новые слова, в которых буква **Ii** читается [ɪ].

Tim [tɪm]		имя мальчика
Bill [bɪl]		имя мальчика
a stick [stɪk]		палка
a pig [pɪg]		поросёнок
little ['lɪtl]		маленький
big [bɪg]		большой

БУКВЫ И ЗВУКИ

Итак, буква **Ii** передаёт два звука [aɪ] и [ɪ].

Прочитай.

[aɪ]	[ɪ]
Mike	Tim
bike	pig
kite	big

Как ты помнишь, буква **Ss** тоже передаёт два звука [s] и [z].

Сравни:

[s]	[z]
cat**s**	bag**s**
kite**s**	flag**s**

В слове **stick** первая буква читается [s], а две последние буквы **ck** стоят рядом, как две подружки, и вместе передают один звук [k].

Скажи:

a stick, a big stick

А теперь посмотри на слова **Bill** и **little**. Видишь сестричек-двойняшек **ll** и **tt**? Они стоят рядышком, но передают только по одному звуку [l] и [t].

Скажи:

        Bill, take a little plate.

1. Назови буквы.

2. Соедини линией одинаковые маленькие и большие буквы.

3. Соедини линией буквы с их звуками. Вот так:

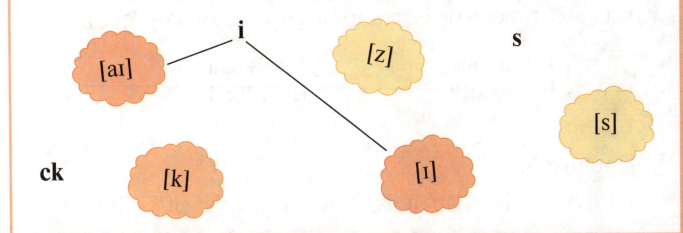

4. Соедини линией слова с картинками.

a pig

Bill

a stick

Tim

ЗАПОМНИ маленькое слово **it**. Ничего, что оно маленькое, оно очень важное. Его можно перевести как **это**. А теперь скажи по-английски:

Это поросёнок.　　　Это кошка.
It is a pig.　　　　　**It is** a cat.
[ɪt ɪz əˈpɪg]　　　　　[ɪt ɪz əˈkæt]

Посмотри внимательно на предложения. Видишь еще одно маленькое слово **is**? Никогда не забывай про него! Когда мы говорим, **is** становится совсем коротеньким:

It's a pig.　　　　　It's a cat.
[ɪts əˈpɪg]　　　　　[ɪts əˈkæt]

5. Прочитай.

　　it it　　is is　　it is　　it is　　it's　it's　it's

6. Прочитай медленно.

It is Tim. It is Bill. It is big Tim. It is little Bill.
It is a pig. It is a stick. It is a little pig. It is a little stick.

А теперь прочитай побыстрее и переведи на русский.

It's Tim. It's Bill. It's big Tim. It's little Bill.
It's a pig. It's a stick. It's a little pig. It's a little stick.

ЗАПОМНИ:

sit [sɪt] — сидеть
still [stɪl] — тихо, смирно
Sit still! — Сиди смирно!

7. Прочитай и переведи.

Tim, sit still!
Bill and Tim, sit still!
Kate, sit still!
Sit still, Jane!

Bill, sit still!
Kate and Jane, sit still!
Little Kate, sit still!
Little Jane, sit still!

ЗАПОМНИ:

маленькое слово **his** [hɪz] отвечает на вопрос **чей?** и означает **его**. Обрати внимание на то, что буква **s** в нём читается [z].
Слово **his** надо говорить тихо, без ударения.

8. Прочитай и переведи.

his pig, his cat, his bike
his stick, his kite, his cap

his bag, his flag, his table
his lamp, his hat, his mat

9. Прочитай слова. Подбери слово к картинке и обведи его кружком. Вот так:

a stick, a pig, (a bat,) a plate, Kate, a cake

a little pig, a big pig, a little stick, a big stick

a little pig, a little cat, a big rat, a big pig

a little table, a big table, a little cake, a big cake

6   I'm Mike

ЗАПОМНИ название буквы **Xx** [eks], которая читается [ks].

Xx	 [ks]

НОВЫЕ СЛОВА

six

a taxi

six [sɪks]   шесть

Max [mæks]   имя мальчика

a taxi [ˈtæksɪ]   такси

Max

ЗАПОМНИ: буквы-друзья **sh** передают звук [ʃ].

sh	 [ʃ]

a dish

a ship

a fish

ВЫУЧИ новые слова с друзьями **sh**.

a dish [dɪʃ] блюдо
a ship [ʃɪp] корабль
a fish [fɪʃ] рыба

1. Прочитай каждое слово по три раза.

six six six   Max Max Max   taxi taxi taxi
fish fish fish   ship ship ship   dish dish dish

ЗАПОМНИ:
множественное число слова **fish** совпадает с единственным.
Сравни:

a fish — six fish
рыба — шесть рыб

2. Прочитай и переведи.

a fish — five fish   His five fish.   His five little fish.
a fish — six fish   His six fish.   His six big fish.

His nine fish. His nine little fish. I like fish.
Cats like fish.

a ship, a fish, a pig, a cat, a bat
six ships, six fish, six pigs, six cats, six bats
six little ships, six little fish, six little pigs, six little cats
six big fish, six big ships, six big pigs, six big cats

ЗАПОМНИ:

множественное число слова **dish** образуется при помощи **es**:

a dish — five dish**es**
[dɪʃ]   [ˈdɪʃɪz]

Звук [ʃ] шипящий, он шипит, поэтому между ним и звуком [z] удобнее произнести [ɪ].

3. Прочитай и переведи.

a dish — five dishes, nine dishes, his big dishes, his little dishes

4. Найди и покажи большую и маленькую букву **Xx**. Назови остальные буквы.

5. Соедини линией буквы с их звуками.

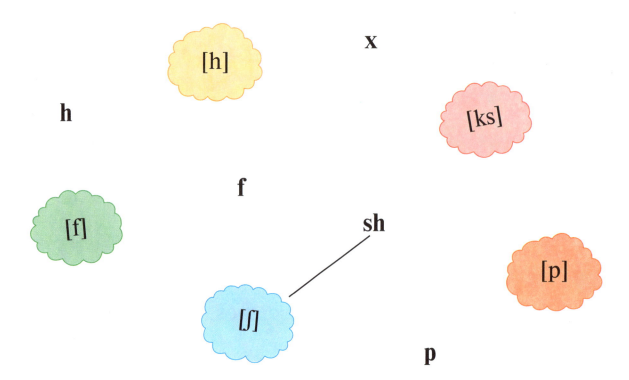

6. Подбери подписи к картинкам. Соедини их линией. Вот так:

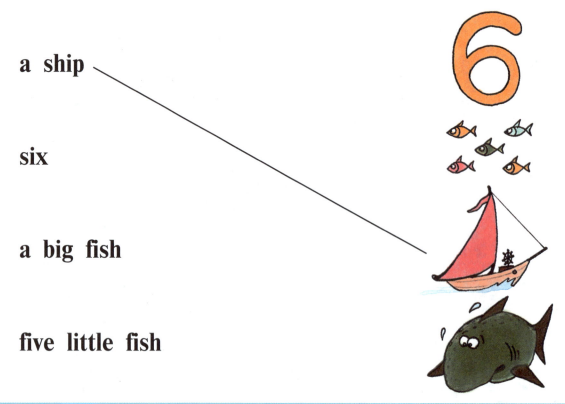

a ship

six

a big fish

five little fish

7. Прочитай слова со звуками [aɪ] и [ɪ].

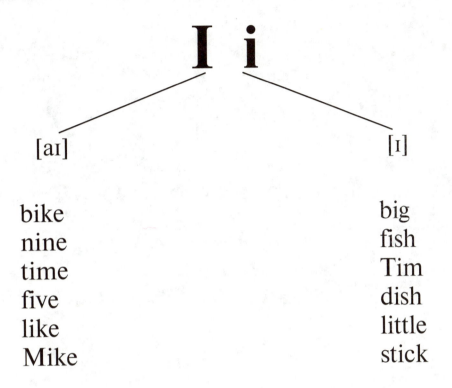

I i

[aɪ]   [ɪ]

[aɪ]	[ɪ]
bike	big
nine	fish
time	Tim
five	dish
like	little
Mike	stick

8. А теперь прочитай слова со звуками [æ], [eɪ], [aɪ] и [ɪ].

[æ]	[eɪ]	[aɪ]	[ɪ]
cat	Kate	kite	dish
bat	take	like	little
cap	Jane	bike	big
mat	make	Mike	Bill

Ты уже можешь сказать, как тебя зовут и сколько тебе лет. Вот так:

I am Mike. I am six. Меня зовут Майк. Мне шесть лет.
I am Kate. I am five. Меня зовут Кейт. Мне пять лет.

Не забывай про маленькое слово **am** [æm], когда ты говоришь о себе. Его можно сказать короче [m], например:

I'm Mike. I'm six.
I'm Kate. I'm five.

9. Прочитай **I'm** несколько раз.

I'm I'm   I'm I'm   I'm I'm   I'm I'm

10. Прочитай и переведи.

I'm Kate. I'm five.   I'm Jane. I'm nine.
I'm Mike. I'm six.   I'm Kate. I like Jane. Hi, Jane!

I'm Jane. I like Mike and Kate.
Hi, Mike! Hi, Kate!
I'm Mike. I like Bill. Hi, Bill! I like Max. Hi, Max!
I'm Bill. I'm five. I like Mike. I like his bike.
I'm Tim. I'm six. I like Bill. I like his kite.
I'm Max. I'm six. I like Bill, Mike, Jane and Kate.

А теперь скажи, сколько лет твоему другу или подруге. Вот так:

Tim is six. Jane is five. Тиму шесть лет. Джейн пять лет. Или покороче: **Tim's six. Jane's five.**

Помнишь маленькое слово **is**? В этих предложениях оно тоже сжалось, но совсем не исчезло.

11. Прочитай и переведи.

Little Tim's six. Little Kate's five. Little Bill's five. Little Mike's six. Big Ben's nine. Big Mike's nine.

12. Прочитай и переведи.

It's a fish. It's a little fish. Nine little fish.

It's a fish. It's a big fish. Six big fish.

It's a ship. It's a big ship. Six big ships.

It's a dish. It's a little dish. Six little dishes and nine big plates.

It's Tim. It's big Tim. Tim, ride a bike. It's his bike. I like Tim. I like his bike. I like his kite. I like his little ship.

It's Mike. It's little Mike. I like Mike. It's his kite. I like his kite. It's his big bike. I like his big bike. It's his fat cat. I like his fat cat. His fat cat's nine.

ЗАПОМНИ:

black [blæk] — чёрный

Six little black cats. I like little black cats.
Six big black cats. I like big black cats.

13. Прочитай, подбери подписи к картинкам и обведи их кружком. Вот так:

six bats, (five caps),
nine little sticks

a fish, a ship,
a bike, a kite

a cat and a rat,
a cat and five rats

a taxi, five fish,
nine dishes

7 Jane likes cakes

ДАВАЙ ВСПОМНИМ БУКВУ **Ee** [iː]

Ты уже знаешь много слов, в которых буква **e** не читается, например: **cake**, **take**, **make**, **bike**, **ride**.
В этом уроке мы поговорим о двух звуках этой буквы [iː] и [e].

ЗАПОМНИ название буквы **Ww** [ˈdʌbljuː], которая передаёт только один звук [w]. Выучи слова, в которых буква **e** читается так, как она называется в алфавите [iː].

Pete

she [ʃiː] она   **he** [hiː] он
we [wiː] мы   **Pete** [piːt] имя мальчика

He и **she** обычно говорят только о людях.

Kate is little.   **She** is little.

Pete is nine.   **He** is nine.

Или покороче:

Kate's little. **She's** little. Pete's nine. **He's** nine.

Когда мы говорим о предметах и животных, знакомое тебе слово it переводится как он, она, оно.

Посмотри внимательно:

His kite is big.
Его воздушный змей большой.

It is big.
Он большой.

His cat is fat.
Его кот толстый.

It is fat.
Он толстый.

И покороче:

His kite's big. It's big. His cat's fat. It's fat.

1. Прочитай слова со звуками [iː] и [ɪ] по два раза.

   [iː]   he   he   she   she   we   we   Pete   Pete
   [ɪ]   his his it   it   it is it is it's   it's

2. Прочитай и переведи.

   It's Pete. Pete's six. He's big. I like his five little fish. It's Jane. Jane's five. She's little. Jane, make a cake. I like cakes, little Jane.

А теперь запомни новые слова, в которых буква **e** читается [e].

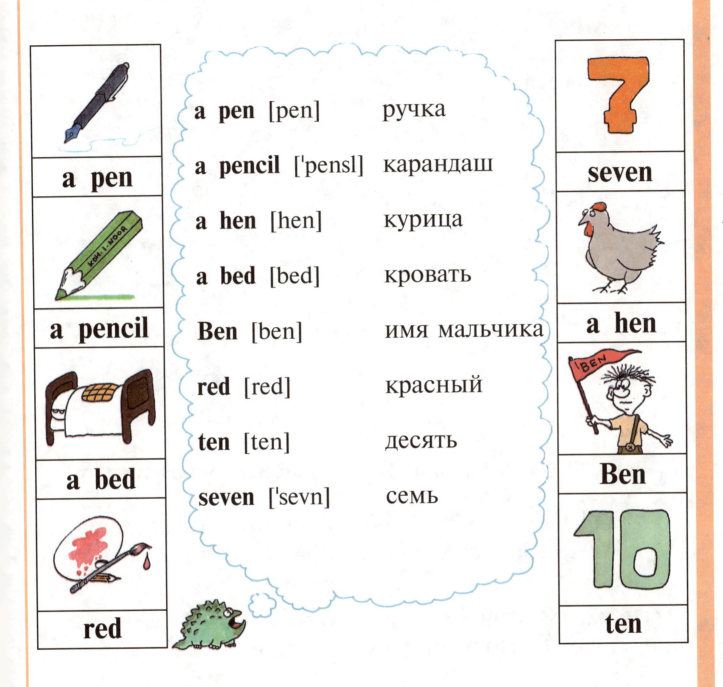

a pen	[pen]	ручка
a pencil	['pensl]	карандаш
a hen	[hen]	курица
a bed	[bed]	кровать
Ben	[ben]	имя мальчика
red	[red]	красный
ten	[ten]	десять
seven	['sevn]	семь

3. Прочитай слова со звуком [e] по два раза.

pen pen   pencil pencil   hen hen   red red
bed bed   seven seven   Ben Ben   ten ten

4. Подбери слова к картинкам. Соедини их линией.

a pen

a pencil

a hen

a bed

red

seven

ten

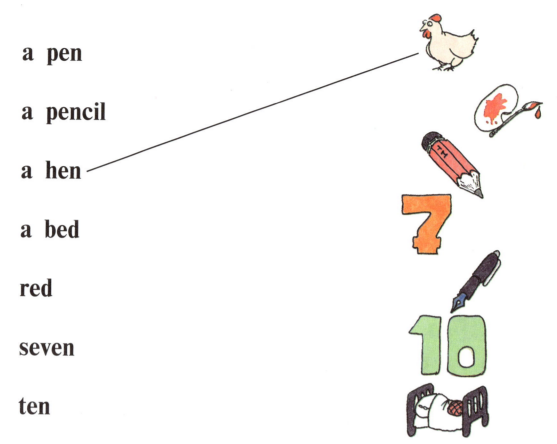

Давай вспомним слово **like** — **любить, нравиться**:

I like his bike.   Мне нравится его велосипед.
We like his bike.   Нам нравится его велосипед.

Ты также можешь сказать, что нравится твоему другу или подруге. Посмотри внимательно:

I like   **но**   He **likes**
We like   She **likes**

Jane **likes** cakes.   She **likes** cakes.
Джейн любит пирожные.   Она любит пирожные.

> Bill **likes** ships.   He **likes** ships.
> Билл любит корабли.   Он любит корабли.
>
> К **like** нужно прибавить **s**, когда мы говорим о том, что нравится **одному** мальчику или девочке или какому-нибудь животному.

5. Переделай и проговори предложения по образцу:

I like pens and pencils.
Tim **likes** pens and pencils.
He **likes** pens and pencils.

We like cakes.
Kate _____.
She _____.

We like big red kites.
Tim _____.
He _____.

I like little red bags.
Jane _____.
She _____.

Cats like fish.
A cat _____.
It _____.

I like black bikes.
Bill _____.
He _____.

We like little bats.
Pete _____.
He _____.

I like big caps.
Max _____.
He _____.

We like black taxis.
Mike _____.
He _____.

ЗАПОМНИ:

swim [swɪm] – плавать
a twig [twɪg] – ветка

a twig

6. Прочитай и переведи.

a twig, five twigs, nine twigs, ten twigs

five pens, six hens, seven pencils, nine beds, five red pens, six black pencils, seven little bags, nine big bats, ten big ships, ten little beds, seven black cats and six red fish

Swim, Kate! Swim, Jane! Swim, Mike! Swim, Bill!

I like pens. He likes red pencils.

We like pens and red pencils.

Jane likes little twigs. Kate likes big twigs.

Take seven little twigs, Jane. Take ten big twigs, Kate.

Max likes his fat cat. His fat cat likes fish. It likes big fish.

I like Max. I like his fat cat.

7. Найди и обведи букву, в названии которой нет звука [i:].

E, P, K, T, D, G, B, C

8　I can swim

ЗАПОМНИ:

если ты хочешь сказать, что ты умеешь что-то делать, тебе не обойтись без слова **can** [kæn].

Например:

> I **can** swim.　　I **can** make a cake.
> Я **умею** плавать.　Я **умею** печь торт.

В этих предложениях звук [æ] в слове **can** становится совсем слабеньким, а иногда и вовсе не произносится [kən, kn].

Прочитай:

> I can ride a bike. I can make a ship.
> I can make a kite. I can swim.
> I can make a cake.

А вот что умеют делать твои друзья:

> We can make ships.
> Мы умеем делать корабли.
> Bill can make a kite.
> Билл умеет делать воздушного змея.
> Kate can swim and ride a bike.
> Кейт умеет плавать и кататься на велосипеде.

1. Прочитай и переведи.

We can make cakes. We can make kites and ships.
I'm Mike. I'm seven. I can swim.
It's Kate. Kate's nine. She can make cakes.
It's little Bill. He's five. He can ride a bike.
It's Tim. Tim's six. Tim can swim and ride a bike.

2. Посмотри на картинки. Прочитай предложения и скажи, кого забыл нарисовать художник.

Kate can make a cake. Max can make a kite. Bill can swim. Tim can make a red flag. Mike can ride a bike. Ben can make a ship.

Всегда веселее делать что-то вместе. **Let's** [lets] поможет тебе предложить друзьям заняться чем-нибудь интересным:

Let's make a cake. Давайте (давай) испечём торт.
Let's ride a bike. Давай (давайте) покатаемся на велосипеде.

А вот так ты можешь предложить свою помощь:

Let **me** make a cake. Давайте (давай) я испеку торт.

ЗАПОМНИ:

me [mi:] — мне, меня

Ты также можешь попросить разрешения что-то сделать:

Let me ride a bike. Позвольте (разрешите) мне покататься на велосипеде.

3. Прочитай и переведи.

Let's swim. Let's make a ship, Ted.

Let's take seven plates. Let me take nine big dishes and five little dishes. Let's take seven cakes and seven dishes.

Let me ride his bike. Let me take his red pencil. Let me take his nine pens and pencils. Let's make a red kite. Let me take his cap. Let me make ten little cakes. Let's take his lamp.

ВЫУЧИ НОВЫЕ СЛОВА

visit ['vɪzɪt] посещать, навещать
send [send] посылать
find [faɪnd] найти, находить, разыскивать
help [help] помогать, помочь

ЗАПОМНИ:

can переводится также **могу**, **можешь**, **можем**, **может**, **можете**, **могут**.

4. Прочитай и переведи.

I can find his bike. Let me find his big bike.
We can help Max. Let's help Max. Let's find his cat. It's black.
We can visit Jane. Let's visit Jane.

Let me help Ben. I can find his ten black hens.

5. Повтори, заменяя выделенные слова на подсказанные.

Пример: Let me find his **bike**. – Let me find his *cat*.

Let me find his **bike**.
cat, cap, bag, pencil, red pen, big black hen, hat

Let's help **Max**.
Kate, Jane, Mike, Bill, Ben, Tim, Pete

Let's send Bill **seven cakes**.
five red pens and six red pencils, ten little ships

9 This is a pen. That's a pencil

Буквы-подружки **th** могут передавать два звука. Посмотри на слова **thin** и **thick**. В них **th** читается [θ]. А в словах **this** и **that** эти же буквы-подружки читаются [ð].

НОВЫЕ СЛОВА

a **thin** pen

thin [θɪn]	тонкий, худой
thick [θɪk]	толстый
this [ðɪs]	этот, эта, это
that [ðæt]	тот, та, то

a **thick** pencil

1. Прочитай каждое слово несколько раз.

thin thin thin   thick thick thick
this this this   that that that

Посмотри на картинку. Кейт стоит у стола, на котором лежат ручка и карандаш. Ручка находится **ближе** к Кейт, и <u>показывая</u> на нее, девочка говорит: '**This is a pen. Это ручка.**' Карандаш лежит **дальше** от Кейт, и <u>показывая</u> на него, она говорит: '**That is a pencil. А вот это — карандаш.**' Как ты помнишь, **is** можно сказать покороче, поэтому после **that** у тебя получится: **That's a pencil.**

2. Прочитай и переведи.

This is a cap. That's a hat.
This is a bag. That's a flag.
This is a table. That's a bed.
This is a kite. That's a ship.
This is a thin pen.
This is a thick red pencil.
This is a thin black cat.
This is a little plate.
This is a big dish.
Bill and his thin hen.
A thin cat and a thin rat.

This is a cat. That's a rat.
This is a ship. That's a kite.
This is a pig. That's a hen.
This is a mat. That's a bat.
That's a thick pencil.
That's a thin black pen.
That's a fat rat.
That's a big plate.
That's a little dish.
A fat cat and a thin cat.
Three thin cats and five thin rats.

Посмотри, Билл хочет познакомить своих друзей.

This is Jane.　　　**This** is Max.
She's seven.　　　**He**'s nine.

Ты видишь, что слово **this** нужно Биллу для того, чтобы показать Джейн и Макса друг другу, познакомить их. Затем Билл говорит **she** про Джейн и **he** про Макса.

Если речь идет о предмете или животном, то после того, как ты на них покажешь, нужно вместо **this** или **that** поставить **it**. Вот так:

This is a bike. **It**'s big. **Это** велосипед. **Он** большой.
That's a cat. **It**'s fat. А вот это — кошка. **Она** толстая.

3. Прочитай и переведи.

This is a bed. It's big. That's a bag. It's little.
This is a pen. It's thin. That's a pencil. It's thick.
This is his ship. It's little. That's his bike. It's big.

This is a cap. It's black. That's a flag. It's red.
This is a pig. It's fat. That's a hen. It's thin.
This is a fish. It's big. That's a dish. It's little.
This is a twig. It's big. That's a stick. It's little.

Если ты хочешь рассказать что-нибудь ещё о девочке или мальчике, сделай это так:

This is Mike. **He** likes ships.
Это Майк. **Он** любит корабли.
That's Kate. **She** can swim.
А вон там — Кейт. **Она** умеет плавать.

4. Прочитай и переведи.

This is Bill. That's Jane.

This is Bill. He's ten.
That's Jane. She can ride a bike.

This is Max. That's Kate.

This is Max. He can make a big red kite.
That's Kate. She can make a cake.

This is Ben. That's Pete.

This is Ben. He can make a big ship.
That's Pete. He can swim.

Тебе уже знакомо маленькое слово **a**. Оно помогает сказать в первый раз о каком-нибудь предмете или животном: о каком-то столе, а не о лампе, о какой-то одной кошке, а не о птичке или собаке. Например:

It's a table. It's a cat.
Это стол. Это кошка.

Если мы хотим сказать что-нибудь ещё об этом столе или об этой кошке, нам на помощь приходит маленькое слово **the** [ðiː, ðə]:

The table's big.
Стол большой.
The cat's fat and black.
Кошка толстая и чёрная.

5. Прочитай и переведи.

It's a pig. The pig's big.   It's a rat. The rat's bad.
It's a hat. The hat's red.   It's a cap. The cap's big.
It's a hen. The hen's thin and black.

ЗАПОМНИ:

маленькие слова **a** и **the** не ставятся перед именами.

Например: It's Ben. Ben's ten.

6. Посмотри, прочитай и скажи, что неправильно на картинках.

It's a pig. The pig's big. The pig's fat. The pig can ride a bike.

This is a big black hen and that's a little pig.

This is a little bed and that's a big table.

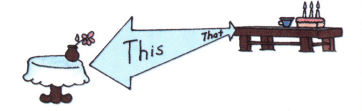

This is a bad rat. That's a little cat.

10 I can see a bee

ЗАПОМНИ:
буквы-сестрички **ee** и буквы-подружки **ea** читаются [i:]. Выучи слова, в которых они встречаются.

НОВЫЕ СЛОВА

ee

a b<u>ee</u> [bi:] пчела

a tr<u>ee</u> [tri:] дерево
gr<u>ee</u>n [gri:n] зелёный

a sw<u>ee</u>t [swi:t] конфета

thr<u>ee</u> [θri:] три

ea

t<u>ea</u> [ti:] чай

m<u>ea</u>t [mi:t] мясо

a s<u>ea</u>l [si:l] тюлень

1. Прочитай каждое слово по два раза.

>   bee bee   sweet sweet   tree tree   three three
>   green green   tea tea   seal seal   meat meat

2. Прочитай и переведи.

I like seals. He likes seals.
This seal's big and that seal's little.

I like tea and sweets. I like tea and cakes.
Jane likes tea and cakes. Bill and Kate like tea and cakes.

Mike likes meat. Kate and Mike like meat.
I like meat.

Bees and trees. Little bees
and big green trees.
I like little bees.
Jane likes green trees.

It's a tree. The tree's green. It's a bee.
The bee's little. The bee likes the green tree.

This is Mike. Mike's seven. Mike can ride a bike.
He can swim. I like Mike.

This is Mike and that's Kate. Kate's nine. Kate can make a cake. She likes cakes and sweets. Mike likes Kate.

Не забывай всегда и везде быть вежливым. В этом тебе поможет волшебное слово **please** [pli:z] **пожалуйста**.

3. Прочитай и переведи.

Please swim, little fish. Please make a cake, Jane. Please take his cap, Bill. Please ride a bike, Max. Please make a kite and a ship, Ben. Please take a sweet, Jane. Please take nine plates, Ben.

4. Соедини линией слова с картинками. Вот так:

a tree

a sweet

a bee

three

tea

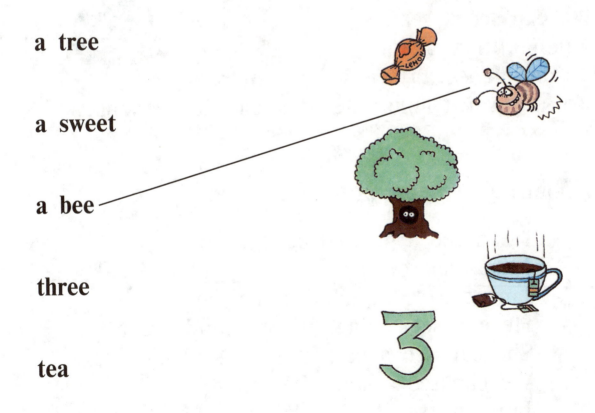

green

meat

a seal

ЗАПОМНИ:

see [si:] — видеть

Ты уже знаешь слово **can** — **уметь, мочь**.
С помощью **can** можно рассказать и о том, что мы видим. Например:

I can see a bee.
Я вижу пчелу.
Mike can see a seal.
Майк видит тюленя.
Kate and Jane can see ten green trees.
Кейт и Джейн видят десять зелёных деревьев.

5. Прочитай и переведи.

> I can see a green tree.
> Mike can see three sweets and five cakes.
> Jane can see a table and a bed.
> He can see a flag. It's red and green.
> She can see a cat. The cat's black.
> We can see a ship. It's big.
> Jane can see five seals.

6. Выучи новые слова.

in	в
eat [i:t]	есть, кушать
read [ri:d]	читать
live [lɪv]	жить
write [raɪt]	писать
well [wel]	хорошо
sea [si:]	море

ЗАПОМНИ:

буквы-подружки **wr** читаются [r].

7. Прочитай и переведи.

Jane can eat three sweets.

Kate can eat seven sweets.

I can eat nine sweets and three cakes.

This cat can eat ten fish.

Tim can write. He can write. Jane can read. She can read. Mike can read and write. He can read and write. We can read and write.

Tim can write well. He can read well. He can swim well. He can make kites well. He likes sweets and cakes. I like Tim.

This is Kate. She can see three seals. She likes seals.

This is Jane. She can see ten green trees. She likes trees.

This is Mike. He can ride a bike well. He likes bikes.

Вот как можно рассказать о том, что обычно **делают** люди и животные.

I swim well.	Я хорошо плаваю.
We make kites.	Мы делаем воздушных змеев.
Cats eat meat and fish.	Кошки едят мясо и рыбу.
Kate and Jane make cakes.	Кейт и Джейн пекут пирожные.

Посмотри внимательно:

Jane and Kate **write** well.	Jane **writes** well. She **writes** well.
Cats **like** meat and fish.	This cat **likes** meat and fish. It **likes** meat and fish.
Fish **live** in the sea.	That fish **lives** in the sea. It **lives** in the sea.

Bill and Max **swim** well.   Bill **swims** well.
He **swims** well.

Ты видишь, что каждый раз, когда мы говорим об **одном** мальчике Билле, об **одной** девочке Джейн, об **одной** кошке или об **одной** рыбке, мы прибавляем букву s к словам, которые обозначают *действия*. Например: write — **writes**, like — **likes**, live — **lives**, swim — **swims**.
Читается эта буква по-разному: [s] или [z].

[s]	[z]
take — takes	read — reads
make — makes	ride — rides
sit — sits	live — lives

8. Прочитай и переведи.

This little fish lives in a big lake.
Bill and Tim swim in this lake.
The little fish likes the big lake.
Bill and Tim like the big lake.

This big seal lives in the sea.
The big seal likes the sea. Seals eat fish.

This is Mike. This is his little cat. Mike likes meat. His cat likes fish. Mike likes his cat. The cat likes Mike.

9. Переделай, как показано в образце, и проговори предложения.

Kate and Jane like tea and cakes.
Bill **likes tea and cakes**. He **likes tea and cakes**.

Tim and Bill like sweets.
Mike _____.
He _____.

Max and Mike make ships.
Bill _____.
He _____.

Ben and Mike make kites.
Max _____.
He _____.

Cats eat fish.
This cat _____.
It _____.

Jane and Kate read well.
Tim _____.
He _____.

Ben and Mike write well.
Pete _____.
He _____.

10. Посмотри на картинки и закончи предложения.

Mike can see three _____.

It's a big green _____.

This is his _____.

11 Fly, my little fly! Bye!

ЗАПОМНИ букву **Yy** [waɪ].
Она передаёт целых три звука!

Сравни:

[aɪ]	[ɪ]	[j]
m**y**	sill**y**	**y**es

The kite is in **the sky**.

Выучи слова, в которых буква **y** читается [aɪ].

a fly [flaɪ]	муха
fly [flaɪ]	летать
the sky [skaɪ]	небо
my [maɪ]	мой, моя, моё

67

1. Прочитай каждое слово по три раза.

   fly fly fly   my my my   sky sky sky

2. Прочитай и переведи.

ЗАПОМНИ:

   says [sez] — говорит
   high [haɪ] — высоко

This is a big fly. That's a little fly.
The big fly says, 'Little fly, let's fly in the sky!'
The little fly says, 'Let's!'
The big fly and the little fly fly high in the sky.

ЗАПОМНИ:

   fly a kite — запускать воздушного змея

My kites **fly** well.
Мои воздушные змеи хорошо **летают**.
My kite **flies** well.
Мой воздушный змей хорошо **летает**.

I can make a kite. I can fly a kite. My kite **flies** well.

The big black fly is in his tea.

Выучи новые слова, в которых **y** читается [ɪ].

happy [ˈhæpɪ] счастливый
silly [ˈsɪlɪ] глупый

А теперь запомни имена мальчиков.

Willy [ˈwɪlɪ]
Andy [ˈændɪ]
Sandy [ˈsændɪ]

Willy

Andy

Sandy

3. Прочитай и переведи.

Willy can read and write well. He helps Andy and Sandy. He says, 'Let's read, Andy! Let's read, Sandy! Let's write, Andy! Let's write, Sandy!' Andy and Sandy read well. Andy and Sandy write well. Willy's happy.

Kate's happy. She can visit Jane. Jane's happy. She can see Kate.

This cat's silly. It's a silly fat cat.

Ты помнишь, как надо поздороваться с друзьями?

Hi, Mike! Hi, Jane!

А теперь ты сможешь попрощаться с ними и сказать: «До свидания!»

Вот так: **Bye!** [baɪ]

4. Прочитай и переведи.

A little fly is in the sky. Fly, little fly! Bye!
Hi, Bill! Hi, Tim! Bye, Bill! Bye, Tim!
Bye, Andy! Bye, Sandy! Bye, Willy!

ЗАПОМНИ множественное число слова **fly**:

a fly – three **flies** [flaɪz]

Three little green flies, five little green flies,
six little green flies, seven little green flies,
ten little green flies.
I can see a fly. The fly's little and green.

Mike can see a fly and a bee. The bee's big. The fly's little. Mike likes the fly. He likes the bee. He says, 'Fly, my big bee! Fly, my little fly!'

This is Willy. Willy can swim and ride a bike. He can make kites. He can fly a kite. His kite is in the sky. It's high in the sky. He can read and write well. Kate likes Willy. Willy's happy.

This is Andy. That's Sandy. Andy's big. Sandy's little. Tim likes Andy. He says, 'Let's visit Andy!' Ben likes Sandy. He says, 'Let's visit Sandy!'

Let's help Billy. Let's find his silly pig. Let's find his seven silly black hens. Pete says, 'Let me help Billy. Let me find his silly pig and his seven black hens. I like Billy.'

5. Прочитай, выучи и разыграй диалог.

Ben: Let's make a kite, Bill!
Bill: Let's!
Ben: Let's fly a kite!
Bill: Yes! Let's!

12 Yes. Yes, it is

Ты уже знаешь слова, в которых буква **y** читается [aɪ] и [ɪ]. Прочитай их ещё раз:

[aɪ]   [ɪ]

my   silly
fly   happy

А теперь запомни слово, в котором **y** читается [j]:

Yes. [jes]   Да.

Без слова **yes** нам не обойтись, особенно когда мы хотим что-то спросить и получить утвердительный ответ. А как задать вопрос? Посмотри внимательно:

It is a green flag.   Is it a green flag?
Это зелёный флаг.   Это зелёный флаг?

Видишь, в вопросе слово is встало перед it.
Они поменялись местами:

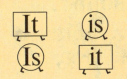

Прочитай предложения и вопросы к ним:

|It|(is) a cat. (Is)|it| a cat? |It|(is) a mat. (Is)|it| a mat?
|It|(is) a tree. (Is)|it| a tree? |It|(is) a lake. (Is)|it| a lake?
|It|(is) a table. (Is)|it| a table? |It|(is) a bed. (Is)|it| a bed?

Можно также спросить:

(Is)|this| a cat?   Это кот?

Ты, конечно, помнишь, что так мы говорим, когда показываем на кота, а если кот сидит подальше, то мы спросим: **Is that a cat?** Обрати внимание: на первом месте стоит **is**, а на втором — **this** или **that**.

Посмотри и прочитай:

|This|(is) a rat. (Is)|this| a rat? |That|(is) a bat. (Is)|that| a bat?

This is a fly. Is this a fly?   That is a bee. Is that a bee?

This is a pen. Is this a pen?   That is a pencil. Is that a pencil?

На эти и другие вопросы, которые начинаются с **Is it ...**, **Is this ...** или **Is that ...**, ты можешь ответить: **Yes** или **Yes, it is**.

Is it a green tree?  Yes или Yes, it is.

Is it a black cat?  Yes или Yes, it is.

Is it a red pencil?  Yes или Yes, it is.

Прочитай:

Is it a red pen? Is this a red pen?
Is that a red pen?  Yes, it is.

Is it a big bee? Is this a big bee?
Is that a big bee?  Yes, it is.

Is it a green kite?
Is this a green kite?
Is that a green kite?  Yes, it is.

Если в вопросе говорится о мальчике или девочке, в ответе нужно сказать **he** или **she**.

Прочитай:

Is **Jane** ten? Yes или Yes, **she** is.

Is **she** ten? Yes Yes, **she** is.

Is **Bill** nine? Yes или Yes, **he** is.

Is **he** nine? Yes Yes, **he** is.

ЗАПОМНИ:

друзья **ch** читаются [tʃ], а подружки **wh** — [w].

ch	[tʃ]
wh	[w]

НОВЫЕ СЛОВА

a **chick**

a **chick** [tʃɪk] цыплёнок
with [wɪð] с
white [waɪt] белый
a **sail** [seɪl] парус
milk [mɪlk] молоко
jam [dʒæm] джем

a **sail**

1. Прочитай и переведи.

Jane can see a little chick. Is Jane happy? Yes, she is.

Is Ben seven? Yes, he is. Is Bill ten? Yes, he is.

Is it a hen? Yes, it is. It's a black hen with five little chicks.

Is this a ship? Yes, it is. It's a big ship with white sails.

Cats like milk and fish.
I like milk. Jane likes milk and jam. Bill likes meat, milk and jam.

2. Задай вопросы, заменяя выделенные слова на подсказанные.

Is it a **lamp**?

lake, rat, mat, cake, bike, kite, pig, stick, table, cap, flag

Is this a **table**?

bed, dish, fish, hen, ship, bat, cat, twig, pencil

Is that a **fly**?

bee, seal, tree, sweet, hat, plate, pen

Is Tim **big**?

little, happy, silly, nine, ten, five, three

> ЗАПОМНИ друзей **all** [ɔːl].

Выучи новые слова, в которых они живут.

a ball

a ball [bɔːl] мяч

tall [tɔːl] высокий

small [smɔːl] небольшой, маленький

3. Прочитай каждое слово по два раза.

    ball ball   tall tall   small small

4. Прочитай и переведи.

Is this a tall tree?   Is that a small tree?   Is Tim tall?
Yes, it is.   Yes, it is.   Yes, he is.

Is Ben small?
Yes, he is.

I'm very tall. Pete's tall. His red ball's small.

Please take a ball. Please take a green ball.
Please take a small green ball.
Pete likes big balls. Jane likes small balls.
I like big and small balls.

Когда нужно сказать, **чей** это велосипед или воздушный змей, мы говорим:

Willy's bike велосипед Вилли
Andy's kite воздушный змей Энди

Видишь, к имени нужно прибавить знак ' и букву **s**. Этот знак называется *апостроф*.
Буква **s** может читаться [s] или [z].

Сравни:

[s]	[z]
Kate's cake	Sandy's cap
Pete's hat	Jane's bag
Mike's ship	Willy's bed

5. Прочитай и переведи.

   I can see a hat. It is Pete's hat. Pete's hat is red.
   I can see a cap. It is Sandy's cap. Sandy's cap is green.
   Mike can make ships. I like Mike's ships.

I like Jane's bag. It's little and red.
Sandy likes sweets. He can eat ten sweets.
Bill likes Sandy's sweets.
He can eat Sandy's sweets and Jane's cakes.

6. В этом рассказе вместо некоторых слов нарисованы картинки. Назови пропущенные слова, тогда ты сможешь прочитать весь рассказ и перевести его.

ЗАПОМНИ:

   nice [naɪs] — вкусный, хороший

This is ![]. Kate's little. She's 5.

Kate's ![] is little. Kate's ![] is little.

Kate's ![] is little. Kate's ![] is little.

Kate can make a ![]. Kate's cake is nice.

This is a ![]. It's Kate's cat. Kate's cat is big and fat.

It's black. Kate says, 'I like my cat.'

This is ![]. Jane likes Kate's big black ![].
She likes Kate's cakes. She says, 'Let's visit Kate!'

13 No, it isn't

ЗАПОМНИ название буквы Oo [əu], которая читается [əu] или [ɔ].

Выучи новые слова. В них буква **o** читается так, как она называется в алфавите [əu].

a sofa [ˈsəufə]	диван
a nose [nəuz]	нос
snow [snəu]	снег
a rope [rəup]	верёвка
a snowball [ˈsnəubɔːl]	снежок
Tony [ˈtəunɪ]	имя мальчика
a rose [rəuz]	роза

81

1. Прочитай каждое слово по два раза.

   sofa sofa   nose nose   snow snow   rope rope
   snowball   snowball   Tony Tony   rose rose

2. Соедини линией слова с картинками. Вот так:

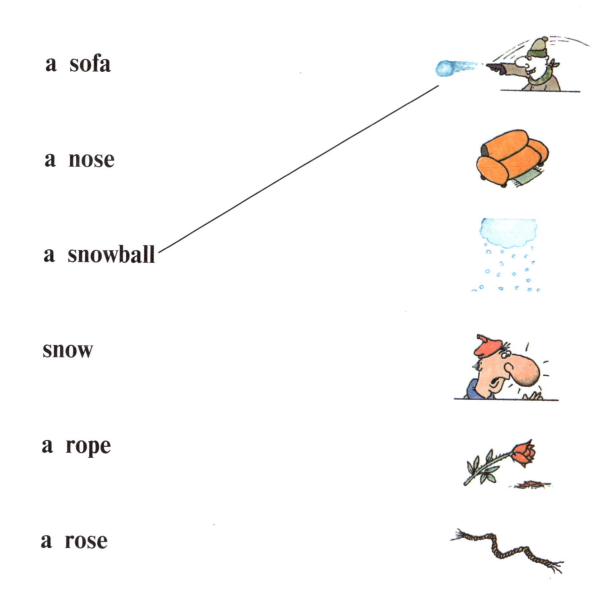

a sofa

a nose

a snowball

snow

a rope

a rose

Мы уже знаем, как можно задать вопросы, например:

Is it a table? Is this a table? Is that a table?

и ответить на них утвердительно: Yes, it is.

Если мы не согласны, мы скажем: No [nəu] или No, it isn't ['ıznt]. Нет.

Is it a pencil?  No или No, it isn't.

Is this a sweet?  No или No, it isn't.

Is that a pig?  No или No, it isn't.

Если в вопросе говорится о девочке или мальчике, в ответе нужно сказать **he** или **she**.

Прочитай.

Is Jane ten? No, she isn't. She's nine.
Is she ten? No, she isn't.

Is Bill seven? No, he isn't. He's nine.
Is he seven? No, he isn't.

3. Прочитай и переведи.

Is it a bed?
No, it isn't. It's a sofa.

Is this a sofa?
No, it isn't. It's a table.

Is that a table?
No, it isn't. It's a lamp.

Is Kate seven?
No, she isn't. She's five.

Is Ben nine?
No, he isn't. He's seven.

Is Jane five?
No, she isn't. She's six.

Is this a pencil?
No, it isn't. It's a pen.

Is that a bag?
No, it isn't. It's a mat.

Is it a fish?
No, it isn't. It's a seal.

Is that a seal?
No, it isn't. It's a fish.

4. Прочитай и подчеркни карандашом правильный ответ.

Is that a rope?  Yes, it is. No, it isn't.

Is it a snowball?  Yes, it is. No, it isn't.

Is this a table?  Yes, it is. No, it isn't.

Is that a rose?  Yes, it is. No, it isn't.

Is that a kite?  Yes, it is. No, it isn't.

5. Прочитай и переведи.

This is a pig. It's a fat little pig. It's silly. Is it silly? Yes, it is.

Is it a chick? No, it isn't. It's a hen. Is it black? No, it isn't. It's white. Is it little? No, it isn't. It's big. It's a big white hen.

Is it a fish? Yes, it is. Is it white? No, it isn't. Is it red? Yes, it is. It's a little red fish. It lives in the sea.

ВЫУЧИ НОВЫЕ СЛОВА

cold [kəuld]   холодный
It's cold!   Холодно!

ЗАПОМНИ:

Когда на улице холодно, мы говорим:
It's cold! Холодно!

Если тебе холодно, ты можешь сказать:

I am cold. I'm cold.   Мне холодно.

Если холодно кому-нибудь другому, скажи:

Mike is cold. Mike's cold.   Майку холодно.
He is cold. He's cold.   Ему холодно.
Kate is cold. Kate's cold.   Кейт холодно.
She is cold. She's cold.   Ей холодно.

Если у тебя или у кого-нибудь из твоих друзей замёрз нос, скажи:

**My nose is cold. His nose is cold.
Kate's nose is cold.**

Нам снова, как и раньше, помогают маленькие слова **am** и **is**.

Вспомни:

I'm six. Ben's seven. He's seven. Kate's little.
She's little. The cat's silly. It's silly.

6. Прочитай и переведи.

It's cold. I'm cold. My nose is cold. My nose is red.

Little Jane is cold. Is she cold?
Yes, she is. She's very cold. Jane's nose is cold.
Is Jane's nose cold? Yes, it is. It's red.

Big Bill's cold. Is he cold?
Yes, he is. He's very cold.
His nose is cold. His nose is cold and red.

ЗАПОМНИ:

буквы-подружки **ay** читаются [eɪ].

ВЫУЧИ НОВЫЕ СЛОВА

a snowman	[ˈsnəumæn]	снеговик
today	[təˈdeɪ]	сегодня
go	[gəu]	идти, ходить
play	[pleɪ]	играть
winter	[ˈwɪntə]	зима

It's winter.

7. В этих рифмовках вместо некоторых слов нарисованы картинки. Назови их, прочитай и выучи рифмовки.

ЗАПОМНИ:

eyes [aɪz] — глаза
so [səʊ] — так, такой

I like it so! — Мне так это нравится!

The cat's eyes.

My 🌨 is so nice!

I like his 🎩. I like his eyes.

I like his 🥕. It's big and red.

My snowman is nice and fat.

It's cold today. Let's go and play!

Let's play in the ❄! I like it so!

14 Let's play snowballs!

ЗАПОМНИ:

буквы-подружки **ey** читаются [eɪ].

ВЫУЧИ НОВЫЕ СЛОВА

old [əuld] — старый
they [ðeɪ] — они
play snowballs — играть в снежки
go home [həum] — идти домой
OK! [əu'keɪ] — Хорошо! Ладно!
Oh! [əu] — О!

1. Прочитай каждое слово по два раза.

   they they   old old   go go   home home

2. Прочитай и переведи текст.

Winter

It's winter. It's cold. Tony and Jane like winter. They like snow. Snow is cold. Snow is white. Snow is nice.
It's very cold today. Tony and Jane can see a hat in the snow. The hat's red and old. Tony says, 'Oh! A nice red

hat! Let's make a snowman!' Jane says, 'No! I'm cold! Let's play snowballs!' Tony and Jane play snowballs. Jane's cold. Jane's nose is red and cold. Jane says, 'Oh! It's cold. I'm cold. My nose is cold. Let's go home!' 'OK!' says Tony. Tony and Jane go home.

3. Прочитай вопросы к тексту и обведи кружком правильный ответ.

Пример: Is it winter?   (Yes, it is.)
                            No, it isn't.

Is snow black?   Yes, it is.
                            No, it isn't.

Is the snowman white?   Yes, it is.
                            No, it isn't.

Is Jane's nose green?   Yes, it is.
                            No, it isn't.

ЗАПОМНИ:

skate [skeɪt] — кататься на коньках

ski [skiː] — кататься на лыжах

carrot [ˈkærət] — морковка

4. Прочитай и переведи.

Mike likes winter. He can ski.
He can play snowballs.
He can make a snowman.
He says, 'Let's play snowballs!
Let's make a snowman.'
Tim likes Mike.
He says, 'Let's help Mike!
Let's find a nice old hat and a carrot, and let's make a big snowman!' Tim's happy.

Little Kate's happy. She can skate.
Jane can ski and skate. Kate says,
'It's cold today. Let's ski and skate!
Oh, I like winter! I like snow! Let's skate and play in the snow!'
'OK!' says Jane. 'Let's!'

ЗАПОМНИ:

буквы-подружки **ng** в конце слова читаются [ŋ].

ВЫУЧИ НОВЫЕ СЛОВА

sing [sɪŋ] петь

bring [brɪŋ] нести, приносить

5. Прочитай каждое слово несколько раз.

| sing | sing | sing | sing |
| bring | bring | bring | bring |

6. Прочитай и переведи.

Let's sing, Kate.
Let's sing, Tim.
Let's sing with Kate and Tim.
Let me sing with Jane.
Let's sing with Jane and Bill.
Please bring me a plate, Jane.
Please bring me a red flag, Max.

Ben's little cat can sing. Ben says, 'Please sing, my little cat.' Ben's cat sings. It isn't silly. It can sing well.

It's winter. It's cold. Tim and Kate like winter. Tim says, 'Let's make a snowman with a red nose!' Kate says, 'Oh, yes, let's! Let me find a carrot!' Kate finds a nice carrot. 'A nice nose!' she says. The snowman's nose is red. Kate likes the snowman's red nose. She likes the snowman. It's so big! Tim's happy.

15 It isn't a sofa

Ты уже знаешь много слов, в которых буква **o** читается [əu]: **a nose**, **a rose**, **Tony**, **snow**.
Выучи слова, в которых буква **o** читается [ɔ].

a dog [dɔg]	собака	
a log [lɔg]	бревно	
a frog [frɔg]	лягушка	
a doll [dɔl]	кукла	
a box [bɔks]	коробка	
a cock [kɔk]	петух	
a fox [fɔks]	лиса	
a clock [klɔk]	часы	

1. Прочитай каждое слово по два раза.

dog dog   frog frog   box box   fox fox   log log
doll doll   cock cock   clock clock

2. Прочитай слова. Подбери слово к картинке и обведи его кружком.

a bag, a flag, (a frog,) a ball, a snowball, a kite

a ship, a clock, a kite, a cake, a lake, a pencil

a cat, a rat, a dog, a frog, a log, a hen, a chick

a sofa, a table, a bed, a box, a pen, a rope

a cock, a log, a snowman, a lake, a fox, a doll

a box, a fox, a log, a frog, a cock, a ball

a hen, a cock, a cat, a chick, a dog, a rat

a flag, a kite, a bag, a doll, a pen, a pencil

3. Прочитай слова.

O o

[əu]   [ɔ]

cold	cock
no	doll
old	dog
nose	frog
rope	fox
snow	box

Предложи ребятам поиграть.

Let's play **tag** [tæg]!
Давайте играть
в салочки!

Let's play **hide-and-seek** [ˌhaɪd ənd ˈsiːk]!
Давайте играть в прятки!

Let's play **hopscotch** [ˈhɔpskɔtʃ]!
Давай поиграем в классики!

Let's **skip** [skɪp]!
Давай попрыгаем через верёвочку!

Можно поиграть и в другие игры.

Let's play **chess** [tʃes]!
Давай играть в шахматы!

Let's play **tennis** [ˈtenɪs]!
Давай поиграем в теннис!

Let's play **hockey** [ˈhɔkɪ]!
Давай поиграем в хоккей!

4. Прочитай, переведи и разыграй диалоги.

ЗАПОМНИ:

hot [hɔt] — горячий, жаркий
It's hot. — Жарко.
late [leɪt] — поздний
It's late. — Поздно.
Fine [faɪn]! — Хорошо!

Jane: Kate, let's play hopscotch!
Kate: OK! Let's!

Tim: Jane, let's play tag.
Jane: OK! Let's!

Bill: Let's play snowballs!
Ben: Oh, no! It's cold!
Let's go home!
Bill: OK! Let's!

Kate: Let's play hide-and-seek!
Jane: Oh, no! It's late!
Let's go home!
Kate: Oh, no! Let's play!

Bill: Mike, let's play tennis!
Mike: No, it's hot. Let's ride a bike!
Bill: Fine!

97

Max: Let's play hockey!
Ben: OK! Let's!

Tim: Let's play chess!
Max: Yes! Let's!

Kate: Let's skip!
Jane: Oh, yes! Let's! I like it!

ЗАПОМНИ:

The cat's **on** the mat.
Кот **на** коврике.

5. Прочитай и переведи рифмовки.

Oh, the cat's on the mat!

Oh, the frog's on the log!

Oh, the cat's in the hat!

Oh, the bee's in the tea!

Oh, the fox is in the box!

Oh, the fish is on the dish!

Ты можешь сказать: **It is a sofa. Это диван.** А можешь сказать: **It isn't a sofa. Это не диван,** если это что-нибудь другое, например, кровать:

Is it a sofa? No, it isn't. It **isn't** a sofa. It's a bed.
Это диван? — Нет. Это **не** диван. Это кровать.

Ты видишь, что тебе помогает в этом **isn't** ['ɪznt]. На самом деле, **isn't** — это два маленьких слова: **is not**, которые часто пишутся и читаются сокращённо — **isn't**:

It **is not** a sofa. = It **isn't** a sofa.

Про девочку или мальчика ты скажешь:

 **Kate is not cold.**
Kate isn't cold.
Кейт не холодно.

**Mike is not late.
Mike isn't late.**
Майк не опоздал.

6. Прочитай и переведи.

Is it a table? No, it isn't. It's a bed.
It isn't a cat. It's a fox. It's a big red fox.
Is it a snowball? No, it isn't. It's a little white ball.
It isn't a black cat. It's a white cat. It's a fat white cat.
It isn't a thin red pen. It's a thick red pencil.
It isn't a flag. It's a kite.
It isn't a fox. It's a big dog.
Is it a frog? No, it isn't. It's a fish.
Is it a cock? No, it isn't a cock. It's a hen.
Is it a bat? No, it isn't. It isn't a bat. It's a frog.
Is it a cap? No, it isn't. It's a hat.
Is it a bee? No, it isn't. It's a fly.
Is it a plate? No, it isn't. It's a dish.
It isn't a seal. It's a fox.
It isn't Mike's ship. It's Sandy's ship.
Is it Willy's bike? No, it isn't. It's Mike's.
Is it Kate's doll? No, it isn't. It's Jane's.
Is it cold? No, it isn't cold. It's hot.
Is Kate late? No, she isn't.
Is Jane cold? No, she isn't cold. She's hot.

16 I've got

Как сказать о том, что у нас есть? В этом нам помогут слова **have got**.

Посмотри внимательно:

I've got a kite and a bike.
(**I've got** = I **have got**)
У меня есть воздушный змей и велосипед.

We've got a kite and a bike.
(**We've got** = we **have got**)
У нас есть воздушный змей и велосипед.

О друзьях нужно сказать так:

They've got a kite and a bike.
(**They've got** = they **have got**)
У них есть воздушный змей и велосипед.

А как сказать о том, что есть у кого-нибудь другого? Посмотри:

He's got a big ship.
(**He's got** = he **has got**)
У него есть большой корабль.

101

Ben's **got** a big ship.
У Бена есть большой корабль.

She's **got** a big doll.
(She's **got** = she **has got**)
У нее есть большая кукла.

Jane's **got** a big doll.
У Джейн есть большая кукла.

Обо всем остальном, если речь идет о ком-то или о чем-то одном, можно сказать так:

The hen's got five chicks.	У курицы есть пять цыплят.
It's got five chicks.	У нее есть пять цыплят.
The ship's got a white sail.	У корабля есть белый парус.
It's got a white sail.	У него есть белый парус.

1. Прочитай и переведи.

   I've got a bag.
   We've got a bag and a flag.
   She's got a bag, a flag and a rope.
   He's got a bag, a flag, a rope and a bike.
   They've got a bag, a flag, a rope, a bike and a ship.

Ты видишь, что в каждом предложении прибавляется по одному слову. Попробуй придумать предложения самостоятельно и поиграть с друзьями в игру '**I've got.**'

Пример:

Kate: I've got a ship.
Mike: I've got a ship and a kite.
Tim: I've got a ship, a kite and a ...

Выигрывает тот, кто назовет больше слов.

2. Закончи рифмовки.

Kate's got a bag.
Jane's got a 🚩

Tim's got a pig.
Bill's got a 🌿

This is a dog.
That's a 🐸

This is a rose.
That's Bill's 👃

Tony's got a chick.
Bill's got a ✏️

Is it a 🏀?
No, it's a little 💧

> ЗАПОМНИ:
>
> **a lot of** [ə ˈlɒt əv] — много
> **long** [lɒŋ] — длинный
> **song** [sɒŋ] — песня

Когда у тебя есть много чего-нибудь, например, кепок, ты можешь сказать: **I've got a lot of caps.** У меня много кепок.

3. Прочитай и переведи.

This is Kate. She's got a lot of dolls. She's got a lot of little flags. She's got a lot of little bags. She's got a lot of little boxes. She's got a lot of pens and pencils. She's got a fat black cat and a little white dog.

That's Bill. He likes winter. He can make a lot of snowballs. He says, 'Let's play snowballs, Pete.'

Tim can sing well. He can sing a lot of songs. He can sing a lot of long songs. He says, 'Let me sing a nice long song.'

17 What's this?

ЗАПОМНИ звук [ə:].

Выучи слова, в которых он живёт.

a **bird** [bə:d] — птица
a **girl** [gə:l] — девочка

a bird

a girl

1. Прочитай каждое слово несколько раз.

bird bird bird   girl girl girl

Ты уже знаешь, как сказать о том, что принадлежит мальчику. Например:

his kite, his ship, his bike, his bag, his cap, his hat, his nose

А вот как можно сказать о том, что принадлежит девочке:

her doll, her ball, her cat, her dog, her plate, her cake

ЗАПОМНИ:

her [hə:, hə] — её

ЗАПОМНИ:

> **what** [wɔt] – что

Ты уже можешь задать вопросы: **What's this? What's that?**, которые означают: **Что это?**

Прочитай.

> What's this? It's a dog.   What's that? It's a cat.
> What's this? It's a frog. What's that? It's a rat.

Ты знаешь, что **this** и **that** мы говорим тогда, когда показываем на людей, животных или предметы, которые находятся близко или подальше от нас.

ЗАПОМНИ:

> **tell me** – скажи мне

2. Выучи рифмовки.

What's this?
It's a flag.
What's that?
It's a bag.

What's that, what's that?
It's a cat in the hat.

What's this? Tell me, please.
It's a bee in the tree.

What's that? Is it a ball?
No, it's a white snowball.

What's this? Tell me, please.
It's a frog on the log.

What's that?
It's a bat in the hat.

3. Выучи новые слова, затем прочитай и переведи текст.

a friend	[frend]	друг
a dress	[dres]	платье
a cage	[keɪdʒ]	клетка
yellow	['jeləu]	жёлтый
often	['ɔfən]	часто
hide	[haɪd]	прятать
give	[gɪv]	давать
then	[ðen]	затем
Spot	[spɔt]	имя собачки
Betty	['betɪ]	имя куклы
Poll	[pɔl]	имя птички

Jane's a nice girl. She's got three friends: Spot, Betty and Poll. Spot's a little black dog. It's very nice. Spot can play with a small red ball. Betty's a big doll. Betty's got big green eyes and a nice red dress. Poll's a little bird. It's a little yellow bird. Poll lives in a big cage. Poll can sing very well. Jane likes Poll's songs. Jane often plays with her friends. She says, 'Let's play hide-and-seek!' and hides Betty. Then she says, 'Find Betty, Spot!' Spot finds Betty. Jane gives Spot a sweet. Spot likes sweets. Jane likes her dog and her bird. She likes her nice big doll.

4. Прочитай и обведи кружком нужные слова.

Например:

Jane is   (a nice little girl.)
        a little cat.
        a little bird.

Jane has got   a doll.
             a bag.
             a flag.

Poll can   swim.
         sing.
         ride a bike.

Jane has got   ten
             five   friends.
             three

Spot can play with   a frog.
                     a ball.
                     a box.

Jane gives Spot   a cake.
                a sweet.
                a fish.

18 I haven't got a kite

ЗАПОМНИ:

друзья **oa** читаются [əu].

Выучи новые слова, в которых они встречаются:

a coat [kəut]   пальто
a goat [gəut]   коза
a boat [bəut]   лодка

1. Прочитай каждое слово по два раза.

    a coat   a coat   a goat   a goat   a boat   a boat

Тебе знакомо маленькое слово **a**, которое помогает рассказать о какой-нибудь любой кошке: **a cat**. У **a** есть друг **an**. Посмотри, какие слова выбирают эти два дружка **a** и **an**. С некоторыми словами удобнее сказать **a**, а с некоторыми — **an**.

Сравни:

a hen   an apple [ən 'æpl]   яблоко

a dog   an ice cream [ən 'aıs kri:m]   мороженое

2. Прочитай, переведи и выучи рифмовку.

This is a little goat in a red coat.

This is an old boat.

Oh, the little goat in a red coat is in an old boat!

ЗАПОМНИ:

буквы-подружки **oy** и **oi** читаются [ɔɪ].

Выучи новые слова, в которых они встречаются.

a boy [bɔɪ]	мальчик
a toy [tɔɪ]	игрушка
noisy ['nɔɪzɪ]	шумный
make noise [nɔɪz]	шуметь
break [breɪk]	ломать

Если тебе старшие не разрешают что-то делать, значит, этого делать нельзя. В этом случае они скажут: **Don't! Не надо!** И ты можешь так сказать кому-нибудь, конечно, если захочешь.

Don't break toys. — Не ломай игрушки.
Don't swim in the lake. It's cold. — Не плавай в озере. Холодно.

3. Прочитай и переведи.

Don't take five cakes, take three. Please give Tim three cakes.
Little boys, don't make noise! Please play chess!
Pete, don't go home. It isn't late.
Kate, don't take that red pencil. Take this black pen.
Sandy, don't play tennis. It's hot. Please go and swim in the lake.
Please don't make a ship, Max. Make a kite.

4. Прочитай слова.

[əu]: snow, snowball, rose, nose, rope, Tony

[ɔ]: dog, frog, log, clock, cock, box, fox

[ɔɪ]: boy, toy, noise, noisy

Как сказать о том, чего у нас нет?

Посмотри внимательно:

I haven't got a bike. У меня нет велосипеда.
(haven't got = have not got)
[ˈhævnt ˈgɔt]

We **haven't got** a kite. У нас нет воздушного змея.

Видишь, теперь нам помогают слова **haven't got**.

Вот как ты можешь сказать, чего нет у кого-нибудь другого, например, у Билла и Майка:

Bill and Mike **haven't got** a bike.
У Билла и Майка нет велосипеда.
They **haven't got** a bike.
У них нет велосипеда.

В других случаях, если речь идет об одном человеке, предмете или животном, нужно сказать **hasn't** ['hæznt] **got**.

Ben **hasn't got** a big ship. (hasn't got = has not got)	У Бена нет большого корабля.
He **hasn't got** a big ship.	У него нет большого корабля.
Jane **hasn't got** a big doll.	У Джейн нет большой куклы.
She **hasn't got** a big doll.	У неё нет большой куклы.
The hen **hasn't got** five chicks.	У курицы нет пяти цыплят.
It **hasn't got** five chicks.	У неё нет пяти цыплят.
The ship **hasn't got** a white sail.	У корабля нет белого паруса.
It **hasn't got** a white sail.	У него нет белого паруса.

5. Прочитай и переведи.

I'm Kate. I've got a big red bag. I've got a red pencil and a green pen in my bag. I've got a big sweet in my bag.

6. Закончи предложения и скажи, чего нет в большой сумке Кейт.

She hasn't got a in her bag.

She hasn't got a  in her bag.

She hasn't got a  in her bag.

She hasn't got a little  in her bag.

7. Посмотри на эту картинку. Прочитай предложения под картинкой. Найди в них ошибки и скажи, что у кого есть на самом деле.

Пример: Mike hasn't got a bike. He's got a kite.

Mike's got a bike. Kate's got a sweet. Jane's got a green bag. Bill's got a little plate with three apples. Tony's got a black cat.

8. Выучи новые слова. Затем прочитай и переведи текст.

a dad [dæd]	папа
Daddy ['dædɪ]	папочка
a little [ə'lɪtl]	немного
clean [kli:n]	чистый
again [ə'gen]	снова
What a fine day [deɪ]!	Какой хороший день!

It's hot today. Mike isn't happy. His dad says, 'Don't ride a bike, Mike. It's hot! Please take a pen and write.'
Mike isn't happy. He says, 'I haven't got a pen! I haven't got a pencil!'
His dad says, 'Please read a little, Mike.'
Mike says, 'It's hot, Daddy. I'm hot! Let's go and swim in the lake!' 'OK!' says his dad. 'Let's.'
Mike and his dad like the lake. It's nice and clean. They swim in the lake. They can see a lot of trees. They can see a lot of fish. They can see a lot of green frogs.
'Don't take the frogs, Mike!' says his dad. 'OK,' says Mike. Mike's happy again. What a fine day!

9. Прочитай и обведи нужное слово кружком. Вот так:

It's cold / (hot) today.

Mike says, 'I'm cold.' / 'I'm hot.' / 'I'm late.'

His dad says, 'Please ride a bike.' / 'Please read a little.' / 'Please go home.'

Mike and his dad swim in the lake. / sing songs. / play hockey.

10. Прочитай предложения и расставь их в том порядке, как они идут в тексте.

Mike and his dad swim in the lake.
Mike's happy.
His dad says, 'Please take a pen and write.'
Mike isn't happy.
Mike says, 'It's hot today! Let's go and swim in the lake!'
It's nice and clean.
They can see a lot of green frogs.
It's hot today.
What a fine day!
Mike says, 'I haven't got a pen. I haven't got a pencil.'
Mike and his dad like the lake.

11. Прочитай и подбери предложения, которые рифмуются.
Соедини их линией. Вот так:

Let's swim in the lake!

It's hot today.

Let's make a cake!

It's got a coat. — Let's go and play!

I've got a goat.

Let's visit Mike!

Let's ride a bike!

19 Have you got a cat?

ЗАПОМНИ букву **Uu** [juː], которая читается по-разному: [juː], [uː] и [ʌ].

Сравни:

[juː]	[uː]	[ʌ]
music	Lucy	cup

Выучи слова, в которых буква **u** читается [juː]:

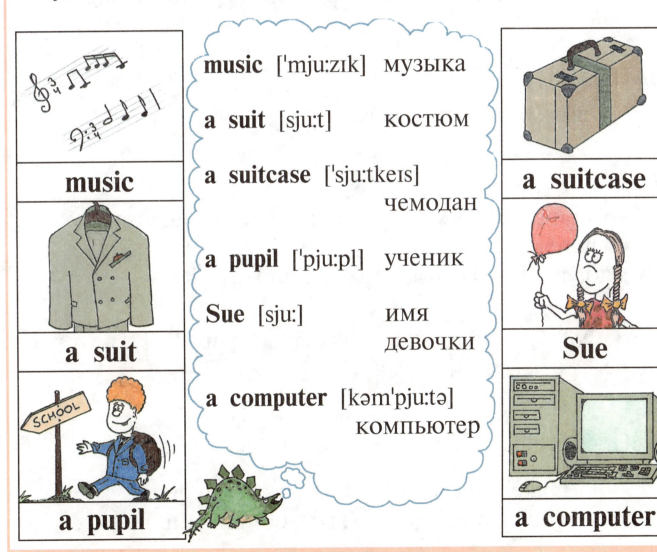

music [ˈmjuːzɪk] музыка

a suit [sjuːt] костюм

a suitcase [ˈsjuːtkeɪs] чемодан

a pupil [ˈpjuːpl] ученик

Sue [sjuː] имя девочки

a computer [kəmˈpjuːtə] компьютер

music

a suit

a pupil

a suitcase

Sue

a computer

1. Прочитай каждое слово по два раза.

> music music suit suit pupil pupil suitcase suitcase
> Sue Sue computer computer

2. Прочитай и переведи.

I like this music. The music is nice. I can sing a song. Let's sing a nice long song.

I like Sue. I like Sue's suit. It's nice. It's red.

Tony's a pupil. He can read and write very well.

Is this a suitcase? No, it's a big bag. It's a big white bag. I like it.

ЗАПОМНИ:

use [ju:z] — пользоваться

Mike, use my bike!
I like computers. I've got a computer. I can use my computer.
I've got a nice red bag. Take it and use it.

ЗАПОМНИ очень важное слово **you** [ju:], которое переводится **ты** или **вы**.

3. Прочитай.

I like sweets.	Я люблю конфеты.
You like cakes.	Ты любишь пирожные.

We like apples.	Мы любим яблоки.
You like ice cream.	Вы любите мороженое.
I can swim.	Я умею плавать.
You can play tennis.	Ты умеешь играть в теннис.
We can play tag.	Мы умеем играть в классики.
You can play hide-and-seek.	Вы умеете играть в прятки.
I can see a fish.	Я вижу рыбу.
You can see a seal.	Ты видишь тюленя.
We can see a tree.	Мы видим дерево.
You can see a rose.	Вы видите розу.
I've got a toy.	У меня есть игрушка.
You've got a pen.	У тебя есть ручка.
We've got kites.	У нас есть воздушные змеи.
You've got ships.	У вас есть кораблики.

4. Прочитай и выучи рифмовки.

I can see a bee.
You can see a tree.

We can read and write.
You can fly a kite.

We can see a cat.
You can see a bat.

I've got a big red bag.   We've got five little pigs.
You've got a big green flag.   You've got five little twigs.

Теперь ты сможешь спросить, у кого что есть. Посмотри внимательно:

Have Tim and Bill **got** a bike?   У Тима и Билла есть велосипед?

Have they **got** a bike?   У них есть велосипед?

Has Ben **got** a bike?   У Бена есть велосипед?
Has he **got** a bike?   У него есть велосипед?

Has Sue **got** a bike?   У Сью есть велосипед?
Has she **got** a bike?   У неё есть велосипед?

Has the hen **got** five chicks?   У курицы есть пять цыплят?

Has it **got** five chicks?   У неё есть пять цыплят?

Has the ship **got** white sails?   У корабля есть белые паруса?

Has it **got** white sails?   У него есть белые паруса?

Ты видишь, что во всех вопросах слова **have** и **has** стоят первыми. А теперь посмотри, как нужно отвечать на вопросы:

Have they got a ship?   Yes, they have. No, they haven't.
Has she got a doll?   Yes, she has. No, she hasn't.
Has he got a bike?   Yes, he has. No, he hasn't.

Посмотри внимательно и запомни:

I have got a bike.   У меня есть велосипед.
Have **you** got a bike? У тебя есть велосипед?

Давай зададим вопрос к такому предложению:

We have got a bike.   У нас есть велосипед.
Have **you** got a bike? У вас есть велосипед?

Не забудь, что **I** и **we** в таких вопросах нужно заменить на **you**.

5. Задай вопросы, заменяя выделенные слова на подсказанные.

Have you got **a pen**?

a pencil, a flag, a cap, a mat, a table, a bed, a dish

Have they got **five chicks**?

a black hen, a red fox, a big dog, a fat cat, a little bat

Has she got **a big doll**?

a green coat, a red bag, a nice hat, a little nose

Has he got **a boat**?

a ship, a bike, a kite, a cap, a coat, a bag

6. Прочитай слова.

[əu]	[ɔ]	[aɪ]	[eɪ]	[ju:]
coat	dog	bike	plate	you
goat	frog	five	late	music
old	fox	my	they	computer
snow	box	fly	play	suit
snowball	clock	Mike	today	Sue

ВЫУЧИ НОВЫЕ СЛОВА

roller skates ['rəulə 'skeɪts]   роликовые коньки
roller skate ['rəulə 'skeɪt]   кататься на роликах
a computer game [kəm'pju:tə 'geɪm]   компьютерная игра

7. Прочитай, выучи и разыграй диалоги.

Mike: Have you got roller skates?
Kate: Yes, I have. I've got nice roller skates.
Mike: Let's roller skate, Kate!
Kate: Oh, yes! Let's!

Tim: Let's play snowballs!
Bill: Oh, no! It's cold.
Tim: I've got a nice computer game. Let's play!
Bill: Oh, yes! Let's!

8. Прочитай и переведи предложения под картинками.

Hi! I'm Kate. I've got a kite and roller skates. I've got a red hat and a red coat. I haven't got a cat. I haven't got a big doll.

Hi! I'm Mike. I've got a kite and a bike. I've got a computer game. I haven't got a ball. I haven't got roller skates. I haven't got a big suitcase.

9. Ответь на вопросы к картинкам.

Has Kate got a ball?
Has she got a kite?
Has she got roller skates?
Has she got a green hat?
Has she got a black coat?
Has she got a cat?
Has she got a dog?

Has Mike got a kite and a bike?
Has he got a coat?
Has he got a computer game?
Has he got a ball?
Has he got roller skates?
Has he got a big suitcase?
Has he got a red cap?

10. Прочитай, переведи и выучи рифмовки.

I can see Mike.
He's got a big bike.

I can see Kate.
She can roller skate.

Has Sue got a nice bag?
No, she's got a little flag.

I can see Ben.
He's got a little hen.
The hen's got a chick.
Has the chick got a fly?
No, the fly's high in the sky.

I can see a tall green tree.
You can see a little bee.
Let's play with the bee.
Oh, no! It's in the tree!

Is Tim tall?
Has he got a little ball?
Oh, yes! He's very tall,
And his ball is so small!

20 Who's this? Who's that?

Ты уже знаешь слова, в которых буква **u** читается [juː]: **Sue**, **music**, **you**. Выучи новые слова, в которых буква **u** читается [uː]:

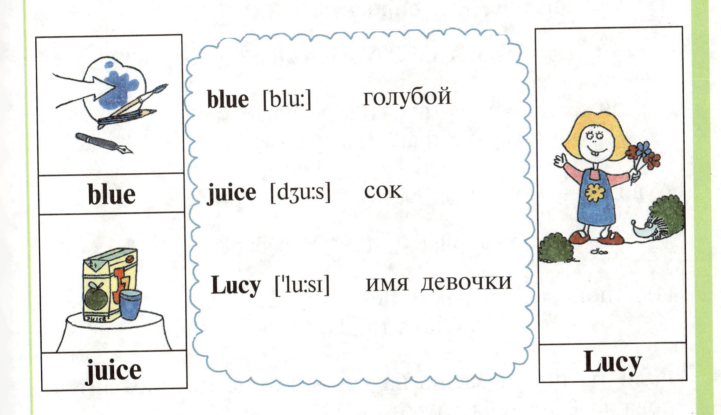

blue [bluː] — голубой

juice [dʒuːs] — сок

Lucy [ˈluːsɪ] — имя девочки

1. Прочитай каждое слово по два раза.

blue   blue   juice   juice   Lucy   Lucy

2. Прочитай и переведи.

Lucy is a nice little girl. She can sing very well. She can skip. She can play chess.
Lucy likes apple juice. She likes sweets. She likes cakes. She likes ice cream and jam.
Lucy's got a nice blue suit. Lucy's got big blue eyes. Ben likes Lucy. She's so nice!

Ты уже знаешь, как спросить:

What's this? What's that? Что это?

Например: What's this? It's a goat.
What's that? It's a coat.

А вот как можно спросить:

Who [huː] is this? Кто это?

Или покороче: **Who's this?**
(Who's this? = Who is this?)

Если ты показываешь на кого-нибудь, кто находится подальше от тебя, нужно сказать:

Who's that?
(Who's that? = Who is that?)

ЗАПОМНИ:

Oh, **I see!** — А, понятно!

3. Прочитай и выучи диалоги.

Tony: Who's this?
Tim: It's my friend Ben.
Tony: Is he nine?
Tim: No, he isn't. He's seven.

Lucy: Who's this?
Sue: It's Kate.
Lucy: Who's that?
Sue: It's Jane.
Lucy: Let's skip with Kate and Jane.
Sue: Oh, yes! Let's!

Daddy: Who's that? Tell me, please.
Pete: It's my friend Mike, Daddy.
Daddy: Oh, I see. He can ride a bike very well.

Kate: Look at that little girl! Who's that, Jane?
Jane: It's Lucy. She's very nice.
Kate: Lucy, what have you got?
Lucy: I've got a little red ball. Let's play!
Kate and Jane: Oh, yes! Let's!

Две буквы-сестрички **oo** читаются [u:] и [u]. Выучи новые слова со звуками [u] и [u:]:

4. Прочитай каждое слово по два раза.

[u]: book book   foot foot   football football
[u:]: moon moon   balloon balloon   spoon spoon
   goose goose

ЗАПОМНИ:

a tablespoon ['teɪblspu:n] — столовая ложка

a teaspoon ['ti:spu:n] — чайная ложка

too [tu:] — тоже, также

look at ['luk ət] — посмотреть на

5. Прочитай и переведи.

Look at this spoon! It's big. It's a tablespoon. Look at that spoon! It's little. It's a teaspoon.

Mike's got a book. The book's thick. Mike likes his book. He often reads it. Mike reads well.

The thick book is Lucy's. The thin book is Tim's. Tim and Lucy read well. They've got a lot of books.

This is a thin book. It's a thin blue book. Don't take it. It is Ben's.

Look at the sky! The moon's in the sky. I like the moon. Balloon, balloon, fly to the moon.

ЗАПОМНИ:

a wolf [wulf] — волк

teeth [ti:θ] — зубы

catch [kætʃ] — ловить

wood [wud] — лес

in good time [ɪn 'gud 'taɪm] — вовремя

This is a big bad wolf. It lives in the wood. It's got big teeth. It can catch hens, cocks and chicks. It can catch goats, too. The wolf can see a little white hen with five chicks. The hen can see the wolf, too. The hen says, 'My little chicks, let's hide!' They hide in good time. The hen's happy. The wolf's so silly!

6. Посмотри на картинку и скажи, кто боится волка.

7. Прочитай слова.

[ɔː]	[æ]	[ɪ]	[iː]	[e]	[u]	[uː]
ball	rat	stick	tea	hen	wolf	spoon
tall	mat	pig	bee	Ben	wood	moon
small	cap	little	seal	pen	book	Lucy

8. Прочитай и переведи.

ЗАПОМНИ:

    a tail – хвост

Lucy is Sandy's friend. She says, 'Let's play a game '**I've got**'.
'What have you got, Sandy?'
Sandy says, 'I've got a football, I've got a balloon, I've got a thick blue book, I've got a computer game. And what have you got, Lucy?'
Lucy says, 'I've got a lot of dolls. I've got three little tables. I've got ten little plates. I've got ten big spoons and ten little spoons. I've got a nice blue suit and I've got a cat.'
Sandy says, 'And what has the cat got?'
'My cat's got a little red nose, two big yellow eyes and a long tail,' says Lucy.

9. Назови, что есть у Сэнди и Люси.

Начни так: Sandy's got ...
                Lucy's got ...

А теперь скажи, что есть у кошки.

Начни так: The cat's got ...

Выбери и обведи кружком, что есть у Сэнди:

a bike, a book, a computer game, a kite, a balloon, a ship, a football

Выбери и обведи кружком, что есть у Люси:

bags, flags, tables, dishes, tablespoons, a dress, a suit, teaspoons, books, dolls

А что есть у кошки? Обведи кружком:

a nose, a coat, a rat, yellow eyes, a cap, a tail

10. Подбери ответы к вопросам. Соедини их линией. Вот так:

Who's this?   Yes, she has.

Has she got
a green coat?   No, she hasn't.

Has she got
a red bag?   It's Jane.

Has she got
a doll?   No, she hasn't.

Who's this?   Yes, he has.
Has he got a kite?   No, he hasn't.
Has he got a dog?   It's Bill.
Has he got a flag?   Yes, he has.

21 I can't swim

Выучи слова, в которых буква **u** читается [ʌ]. Запомни также название буквы **Zz** [zed], которая передаёт звук [z].

a cup	[kʌp]	чашка
a tub	[tʌb]	ванна
a duck	[dʌk]	утка
a nut	[nʌt]	орех
the sun	[sʌn]	солнце
a puppy	[ˈpʌpɪ]	щенок
Liz	[lɪz]	имя девочки
a zebra	[ˈziːbrə]	зебра

1. Прочитай каждое слово по два раза.

  cup cup duck duck nut nut sun sun
  tub tub puppy puppy Liz Liz zebra zebra

2. Прочитай и переведи.

ЗАПОМНИ:

  And you? — А ты?

  Let's have tea! — Давайте выпьем чаю!

  It's fun [fʌn]**!** — Это весело!

  a stripe [straɪp] — полоса

Look at this cup! It's nice and blue. I like it. And you? Let's have tea!

This is a goose, and that's a duck. The goose is white, the duck is black. The goose can fly. The duck can fly, too. They can fly high in the sky.

What's this? Is it a little apple? No, it isn't. It isn't an apple. It's a big nut. Liz likes nuts and apples.

Look at this puppy! It's black and white. It's very nice. It can play with a little yellow ball. It likes sweets.

This is a big tub. It's nice and clean. Little Liz can swim in it.

This is a zebra. It's got black and white stripes. It's very nice.

The sun is in the sky. It's very hot. I like the sun.

Познакомься со звуком [ɑ:]. Выучи слова, в которых он живёт:

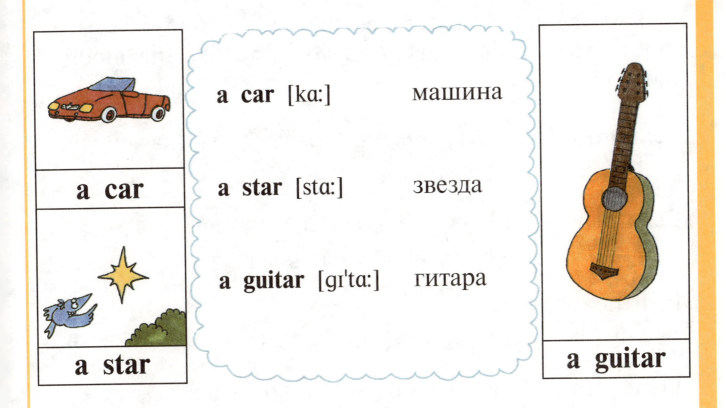

3. Прочитай каждое слово несколько раз.

car car car   star star star   guitar guitar guitar

ЗАПОМНИ:

play the guitar — играть на гитаре
together [tə'geðə] — вместе

4. Прочитай и переведи.

Max likes music. He can sing very well. He can play the guitar. Mike and Lucy like music, too. They can sing a lot of songs. Let's sing together! It's fun!

Tim's got a lot of cars. Ben often plays with Tim. He often plays with his cars. Ben likes Tim's cars. 'Let's play together,' he says. 'It's fun!'

Look at the sky! You can see the moon. You can see a lot of stars. I like stars. And you? We like the moon. And you?

Если ты, например, умеешь плавать, ты скажешь:

I can swim.

Если ты не умеешь плавать, ты скажешь:

I cannot [ˈkænət] **swim.**

Или покороче:

I can't [kɑːnt] **swim.**

Если кто-нибудь не может что-то сделать, нужно сказать так:

Lucy can't help Bill.
Люси не может помочь Биллу.
I can't visit Kate.
Я не могу навестить Кейт.

5. Прочитай и переведи.

Mike can see his car.
Bill can find his puppy.
Kate can see that star.
Jane can play the guitar.
Sue can find her ducks.

Mike can't see his car.
Bill can't find his puppy.
Kate can't see that star.
Jane can't play the guitar.
Sue can't find her ducks.

Tim can play hopscotch. Tim can't play hopscotch.
Pete can use a computer. Pete can't use a computer.
Ben can visit Max. Ben can't visit Max.

6. Выучи новые слова. Затем прочитай и переведи текст.

when [wen]	когда
but [bət]	но
to play football	играть в футбол
good [gud]	хороший
Good! [gud]	Хорошо!

My friends

Mike is my good friend. Sue is my good friend, too.
Mike can ride a bike. He can play football very well. He can't play tennis but he can swim. He can't play chess but he can fly a kite. He can read but he can't write well. I like Mike.

Sue is nice. She can't play the guitar but she can sing. She can sing nice songs. She can't play chess very well but she can play computer games. I like Sue.

I often play with Mike and Sue.

Mike and Sue often make noise. I often make noise, too. When Mike, Sue and I make noise my Daddy says, 'Don't make noise, Mike and Sue! Don't make noise, Tony! Don't break toys! I can't read my book. Please go and play a computer game!' 'OK,' says Mike. 'OK,' says Sue.

I've got a lot of nice computer games. We play and play. Then Sue says, 'It's late. Let's go home, Mike!'

I say, 'Oh, no! Please don't go! Let's play hide-and-seek!' 'Oh, good!' says Sue. And we play and play...

7. Скажи, что умеют или не умеют делать дети. Начни так:

        Mike can ...   Sue can ...
        Mike can't ...   Sue can't ...

8. Прочитай, переведи и выучи диалоги.

ЗАПОМНИ:

    only ['əunlɪ] — только

Kate: Who's this?
Jane: It's Mike. He can't fly a kite but he can ride a bike.
Kate: Oh, good!

Lucy: Mike's got a lot of computer games.
Sue: Let's play with Mike!
Lucy: Oh, yes! Let's! I can't play chess but I can play computer games.

Tim: Look! Ben can use a computer.
Bill: No, he can't. He can only play computer games.

22 Can you swim?

Как спросить: «Ты умеешь плавать?» Посмотри внимательно:

Can you swim?

Ты видишь, что, когда мы хотим задать вопрос, слово **can** становится на первое место, а вместо **I** или **we** нужно сказать **you**.

А как ответить на этот вопрос?

Can you swim?   **Yes** или **Yes, I can.**
No или **No, I can't.**

Давай ответим на другие вопросы. Прочитай.

Can you play chess?   **Yes** или **Yes, I can.**
No или **No, I can't.**

Can Mike and Sue play tag?   **Yes** или **Yes, they can.**
No или **No, they can't.**

Can they play tag?	**Yes** или **Yes, they can.** **No** или **No, they can't.**
Can Mike play hide-and-seek?	**Yes** или **Yes, he can.** **No** или **No, he can't.**
Can he play hide-and-seek?	**Yes** или **Yes, he can.** **No** или **No, he can't.**
Can Jane skip?	**Yes** или **Yes, she can.** **No** или **No, she can't.**
Can she skip?	**Yes** или **Yes, she can.** **No** или **No, she can't.**
Can a duck fly?	**Yes** или **Yes, it can.**
Can a cat fly?	**No** или **No, it can't.**

1. Задай вопросы, заменяя выделенные слова на подсказанные.

Can you **write**?

ride a bike, swim, make a cake, play a computer game

Can she **play tag**?

play hopscotch, play the guitar, play with a ball

Can he **swim**?

fly a kite, read and write, ride a bike, play chess

2. Выучи новые слова. Затем прочитай и переведи текст.

ask [ɑ:sk]	спрашивать
answer [ˈɑ:nsə]	отвечать
run [rʌn]	бегать
children [ˈtʃɪldrən]	дети

What's in my bag?

Jane's got a big green bag. She asks, 'What's in my bag?'
'Is it a red apple?' asks Tim.
'No,' answers Jane. 'It isn't a red apple.'
'Is it a white rat? Can it run?' asks Lucy.
'No,' answers Jane. 'It isn't a white rat. It can't run.'
'Is it a little bird? Can it fly?' asks Bill.
'No,' says Jane. 'It isn't a bird and it can't fly.'
'Can you play with it?' asks Tim.
'Yes, I can,' says Jane.
'Is it a big red ball?' asks Tim.
'Yes, it is. It's a big red ball,' says Jane. 'Let's play!'
'Oh, yes! Let's!' answer the children.

3. Прочитай и обведи кружком, что оказалось у Джейн в сумке.

a computer game, a balloon, a puppy, a ball, a flag, a sweet

4. Прочитай слова.

[ə:]: a bird, a girl, her
[ɑ:]: a car, a star, a guitar, ask, answer
[ʌ]: a cup, a tub, a puppy, the sun, run
[eɪ]: a cake, they, a game, play, take
[əu]: snow, a snowball, a rose, a nose

Ты уже почти умеешь считать до десяти. Запомни ещё несколько цифр:

one [wʌn] — один
two [tu:] — два
four [fɔ:] — четыре
eight [eɪt] — восемь

5. Посчитай.

1 2 3 4 5 6 7 8 9 10
one two three four five six seven eight nine ten

6. А теперь посчитай в обратном порядке и выучи рифмовку.

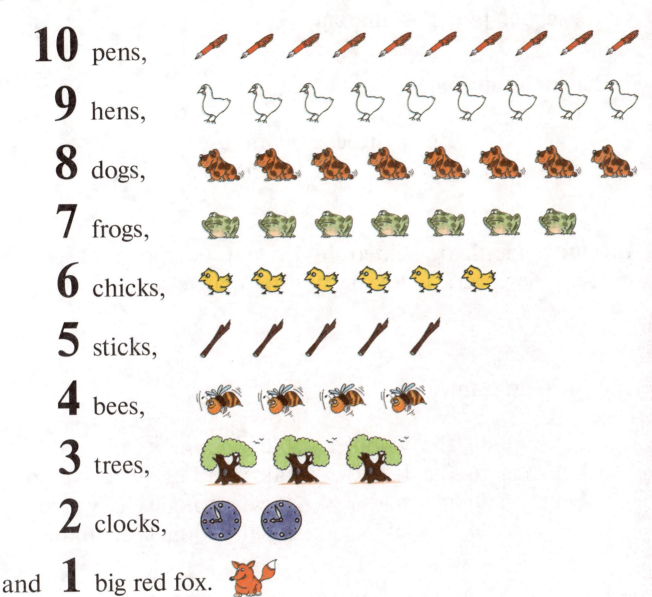

10 pens,
9 hens,
8 dogs,
7 frogs,
6 chicks,
5 sticks,
4 bees,
3 trees,
2 clocks,
and **1** big red fox.

ЗАПОМНИ:

буквы-подружки **ou** читаются [au].

Выучи слова, в которых они живут:

a mouse [maus] — мышь
a house [haus] — дом

a mouse

a house

ЗАПОМНИ:

grey [greɪ] — серый
school [skuːl] — школа

7. Выучи рифмовку.

I'm a little grey mouse.
I live in this big house.

Выучи маленькое слово to [tu, tə], **которое отвечает на вопрос куда? и указывает направление.**

Прочитай и запомни:

Let's go **to** the wood!	Давай пойдем **в** лес!
Let's go **to** the lake!	Давай пойдем **на** озеро!
Let's go **to** the sea!	Давай пойдем **к** морю!
Let's go **to** school!	Давай пойдем **в** школу!

8. Прочитай, переведи и разыграй диалог.

Cat: Little mouse, let's play! Let's play tag!
Mouse: Oh, no! You can catch me! Let's go to the wood and play hide-and-seek!
Cat: Oh, yes! Let's! Let's go to the wood!
Mouse: Can you find me, silly cat? No, you can't! I can hide in my house. You can't find me! You can't catch me! Bye!

23 We are children

ЗАПОМНИ звук [ɛə]. Выучи слова, в которых он живёт:

a chair

a **bear** [bɛə]	медведь
a **hare** [hɛə]	заяц
a **chair** [tʃɛə]	стул
a **pear** [pɛə]	груша

a hare

Познакомься с буквой **Qq** [kjuː], она неразлучна с подружкой **u**. Запомни: **qu** читается [kw].

a **squirrel** [ˈskwɪrəl] — белочка

1. Прочитай каждое слово несколько раз.

bear bear bear   hare hare hare   pear pear pear
chair chair chair   squirrel squirrel squirrel

2. Прочитай и переведи.

ЗАПОМНИ:

    brown [braun] — коричневый
    short [ʃɔːt] — короткий
    soft [sɔft] — мягкий

I can see a bear and a hare. The bear's big and brown. The hare's little and white. The bear hasn't got a long tail. The hare hasn't got a long tail. They've got short tails.

A little squirrel often sits in the green tree. The tree is tall. The squirrel has got a lot of nuts. It likes nuts.

Tony's cat often sits on a little chair. The cat likes the chair. It's nice and soft.

This is an apple. That's a pear. The apple is big and red. The pear is nice and yellow. Children like apples and pears.

ЗАПОМНИ: у одной мамы, которую зовут **BE** [biː] — **быть**, есть три сына: **AM**, **IS** и **ARE**. Двоих ты уже знаешь. Они дружат с единственным числом.

Например:

    I **am** a boy.   She **is** a girl.

А третий сын, **ARE** [ɑː, ə], дружит со множественным числом и со словом **you**.

Сравни:

You're my friend. (You're = you are) Ты мой друг.	You're my friends. Вы мои друзья.

Посмотри и прочитай:

We're happy. Мы счастливы.
(We're = we are)

They're children. Они дети.
(They're = they are)

Tim and Kate **are** pupils. Тим и Кейт – ученики.
Cats **are** nice and soft. Кошки хорошие и мягкие.

Все три брата живут дружно, никогда не ссорятся и не расстраивают маму **BE**.

А как задать вопрос с маленьким словом **are**? Посмотри:

You **are** my friend.   **Are** you my friend?
You **are** my friends.   **Are** you my friends?
They **are** girls.   **Are** they girls?

Ты видишь, что во всех вопросах **are** стоит первым.

А как ответить на эти вопросы? Посмотри внимательно и запомни:

Are you my friend? **Yes** или **Yes, I am.**
No или **No, I'm not.**
(I'm not = I am not)

Are you my friends? **Yes** или **Yes, we are.**
No или **No, we aren't.**
(we aren't = we are not)

А теперь запомни вопросы к таким предложениям:

I'm a pupil.
(I'm = I am)
Я ученик.

Are you a pupil?
Ты ученик?

We are pupils.
Мы ученики.

Are you pupils?
Вы ученики?

Tim and Kate are pupils.
Тим и Кейт ученики.

Are Tim and Kate pupils?
Тим и Кейт ученики?

Cats are nice and soft.

Are cats nice and soft?
Кошки хорошие и мягкие?

Прочитай, как нужно ответить на эти вопросы:

Are you a pupil?	**Yes** или **Yes, I am.** **No** или **No, I'm not.** (I'm not = I am not)
Are you pupils?	**Yes** или **Yes, we are.** **No** или **No, we aren't.** (we aren't = we are not)
Are Tim and Kate pupils?	**Yes** или **Yes, they are.** **No** или **No, they aren't.** (they aren't = they are not)
Are cats nice and soft?	**Yes** или **Yes, they are.** **No** или **No, they aren't.**

3. Выучи рифмовки, чтобы хорошенько запомнить трёх братьев **am**, **is** и **are**.

ЗАПОМНИ:

a name [neɪm] — имя

I'**m** a girl.
You **are** a boy.
I've got a cat.
You've got a toy.

We **are** girls.
You **are** boys.
We've got cats.
You've got toys.

He **is** a boy.
His name is Bill.
'Little Bill, please sit still!'

She **is** a girl.
Her name's Sue.
She likes cats. And you?

Tim and Bill are little boys.
They have got a lot of toys.
They can make a lot of noise.
They are happy little boys.

4. Выучи новые слова. Затем прочитай и переведи текст.

hop [hɔp]	скакать
every [ˈevrɪ]	каждый
an evening [ˈiːvnɪŋ]	вечер
a heron [ˈherən]	цапля
beautiful [ˈbjuːtɪful]	красивый
grass [grɑːs]	трава
think [θɪŋk]	думать
a hole [həul]	норка
catch [kætʃ]	поймать
under [ˈʌndə]	под
lucky [ˈlʌkɪ]	удачливый

I'm a little green frog. I can sing and swim very well. I can hop. This is my lake. It's nice, clean and blue. I live in this lake. I eat little green flies. They are very nice. They fly in the sky.

Every evening I sit on my log and sing long songs, 'Oh, my clean and beautiful lake! Oh, my little green flies!'

A tall white heron likes the lake, too. The heron is beautiful but so silly! It's got two long legs and a long red nose. It likes fish. It likes frogs. It likes me.

The heron says, 'Hi, little frog! Let's play!'

'OK, let's! Let's play hide-and-seek. Find me!' I hide. The heron thinks, 'Is it on the log? No, it isn't. Is it in the grass? No, it isn't.'

But I'm in a little hole under the log. The heron can't see me. The heron can't catch me. It's fun! The silly heron isn't happy. I'm lucky.

5. Что умеет делать лягушонок?
Прочитай и обведи кружком:

it can sing, it can ride a bike,
it can hop, it can play chess,
it can swim, it can fly a kite

Во что играли лягушонок и цапля?
Обведи кружком:

hopscotch, tennis, tag, hide-and-seek, hockey

Где спрятался лягушонок?
Обведи кружком:

under the tree, in the hat, in a little hole under the log, in the lake, in the grass

6. Прочитай, выучи и разыграй диалоги.

ЗАПОМНИ:

a park [pɑ:k] — парк

Kate: Let's go to the wood, Jane!
Jane: Let's! It's so hot!

Tim: Let's go to the lake! It's so hot!
Bill: Oh, yes! Let's go with my dad! I can't swim.
Tim: OK!

Sue: Let's go to school!
Pete: Oh, no! Let's play in the park!

Max: I like winter! Let's go to the lake and skate.
Lucy: Oh, no! It's cold! Let's play a computer game!
Max: OK! Let's!

Kate: Let's go to the sea!
Sue: Can you swim?
Kate: Oh, yes! I can swim very well!
Sue: Oh, good! Let's go with my dad!

24 Do you read well?

ЗАПОМНИ друзей **ph**, которые читаются [f]. Выучи новые слова с этими буквами:

a photo

a dolphin [ˈdɔlfɪn] дельфин

an elephant [ˈelɪfənt] слон

a telephone [ˈtelɪfəun] телефон

Phil [fɪl] имя мальчика

a photo [ˈfəutəu] фотография

Phil

1. Прочитай каждое слово по три раза.

dolphin	elephant	photo	telephone	Phil
dolphin	elephant	photo	telephone	Phil
dolphin	elephant	photo	telephone	Phil

153

2. Прочитай и переведи.

ЗАПОМНИ:

all [ɔːl] — все

carry [ˈkærɪ] — носить

heavy [ˈhevɪ] — тяжёлый

quickly [ˈkwɪklɪ] — быстро

I can see two dolphins. They live in the sea. They are very nice. They can swim and play with a ball. All children like dolphins. I like dolphins, too.

This is a big elephant. It's big and grey. That's a little elephant. It's grey, too. The big elephant can carry logs. The little elephant can run but it can't carry heavy logs.

This is an elephant. That's a zebra. The zebra has got black and white stripes. It can run very quickly. The elephant can run quickly, too.

Look at this photo! You can see my friend Phil in it. You can see a nice little dolphin, too. It's a beautiful photo. Phil and the dolphin are very happy! They are good friends.

3. Соедини линией слова с картинками.

a telephone

an elephant

a photo

a dolphin

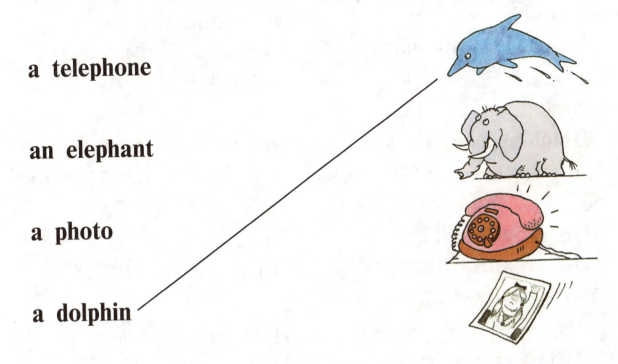

Ты уже знаешь, как сказать:

I'm a pupil.	Я ученик.
I can swim.	Я умею плавать.
I've got a pen.	У меня есть ручка.

Ты также знаешь, как задать вопросы к этим предложениям и ответить на них:

Are you a pupil?	Yes, I am или No, I'm not.
Can you swim?	Yes, I can или No, I can't.
Have you got a pen?	Yes, I have или No, I haven't.

А как задать другие вопросы?
Прочитай и посмотри внимательно:

| **You read well**. | **Do** you read well? |
| Ты хорошо читаешь. | Ты хорошо читаешь? |

Bill and Mike often play football.
Билл и Майк часто играют в футбол.

Do Bill and Mike often play football?
Билл и Майк часто играют в футбол?

Dolphins like the sea.
Дельфины любят море.

Do dolphins like the sea?
Дельфины любят море?

He reads well.
Он хорошо читает.

Does he read well?
Он хорошо читает?

Pete runs very quickly.
Пит быстро бегает.

Does Pete run very quickly?
Пит быстро бегает?

This little dolphin likes the sea.
Этот маленький дельфин любит море.

Does this little dolphin like the sea?
Этот маленький дельфин любит море?

The wolf lives in the wood.
Волк живёт в лесу.

Does the wolf live in the wood?
Волк живёт в лесу?

This seal lives in the sea.
Этот тюлень живёт в море.

Does this seal live in the sea?
Этот тюлень живёт в море?

Ты видишь, что эти вопросы не могут обойтись без двух помощников **do** [duː] и **does** [dʌz]. С единственным числом всегда дружит **does**, а **do** помогает множественному числу и словам **you** и **I**.
В вопросах **do** и **does** всегда стоят на первом месте.

А как ответить на эти вопросы?
Посмотри внимательно:

Do you read well?
Yes, **I do** или No, **I don't**. (don't [dəunt] = do not)

Do Bill and Mike often play football?
Yes, they **do** или No, they **don't**.

Do dolphins like the sea?
Yes, they **do** или No, they **don't**.

Does he read well?
Yes, he **does** или No, he **doesn't**.
(doesn't = does not)

Does this little dolphin like the sea?
Yes, it **does** или No, it **doesn't**.

Does the wolf live in the wood?
Yes, it **does** или No, it **doesn't**.

Does this seal live in the sea? Yes, it **does** или
No, it **doesn't.**

Ты также можешь дать полные ответы.
Прочитай:

Do you read well? Yes, **I do**. I read well
или No, **I don't**. **I don't** read well.

Does he read well? Yes, he **does**. He reads well
или No, he **doesn't**. He **doesn't** read well.

Do cats like fish? Yes, they **do**. They like fish
или No, they **don't**. They **don't** like fish.

4. Прочитай и переведи.
Назови и подчеркни карандашом краткий ответ одной чертой, а полный ответ двумя чертами.

Do seals live in the sea?

    Yes, they do.
    Yes, they do. Seals live in the sea.

Do frogs live in the sea?

    No, they don't.
    No, they don't. Frogs don't live in the sea.

Do dolphins live in the lake?

    No, they don't.
    No, they don't. Dolphins don't live in the lake.

Does the elephant eat fish?

    No, it doesn't.
    No, it doesn't. The elephant doesn't eat fish.

Does Tim like ice cream?

    Yes, he does.
    Yes, he does. Tim likes ice cream.

Do you like sweets?

    Yes, I do.
    Yes, I do. I like sweets.

Does she play chess?

    No, she doesn't.
    No, she doesn't. She doesn't play chess.

Does Kate play the guitar?

    Yes, she does.
    Yes, she does. Kate plays the guitar.

5. Соедини линией слова, противоположные по значению.
Вот так:

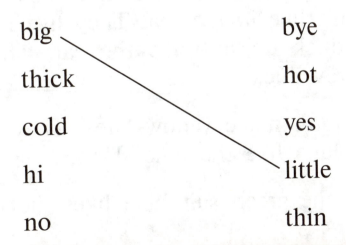

6. Ты уже знаешь разные цвета. Посмотри на картинку и назови цвета кубиков, в которые играют дети.

7. Прочитай и переведи.

Does Kate like yellow chicks?   Yes, she does.
Do black and white zebras like fish?   No, they don't.

This white cat doesn't like milk. It likes fish.
Brown bears don't live in the sea. They live in the wood.
The little grey duck doesn't like the cat. The black cat likes the little grey duck.

Mike and Tim don't make yellow kites. They make white kites. Kate and Jane like the blue sky.

Sue doesn't like the green suit. She likes the red dress.

25 I want to skate. He likes to play

Ты знаешь, как сказать, что тебе или кому-нибудь другому кто-то или что-то нравится. Например:

I like ice cream.

Mike likes kites and ships.

Cats like milk and fish.

Sandy likes Sue.

They like tea and cakes.

Squirrels like nuts.

А вот как можно сказать о том, что мы любим делать. Посмотри:

We **like to swim**.   Мы любим плавать.
I **like to play tennis**.   Я люблю играть в теннис.
Ben **likes to play chess**.   Бен любит играть в шахматы.

Tim and Bill **like to fly** kites.
Тим и Билл любят запускать воздушных змеев.

They **like to swim**.
Они любят плавать.

Ты также можешь сказать о том, что **хочешь** делать ты или твои друзья. В этом тебе поможет слово **want** [wɔnt] — **хотеть**.

Например:

I want to play chess.	Я хочу играть в шахматы.
He wants to skate.	Он хочет кататься на коньках.
They want to go to the wood.	Они хотят пойти в лес.
Bill and Mike want to swim.	Билл и Майк хотят плавать.
You want to ski.	Ты хочешь кататься на лыжах.

Ты знаешь, как можно сказать о животных, когда им что-нибудь или кто-нибудь нравится:

My dog likes my dad. My dog likes sweets.
Sue's got a cat. The cat likes Sue.
Sue's cat likes milk and fish.

А теперь запомни, как можно рассказать о том, что они **любят** или **хотят** делать. Например:

My dog likes to play with a ball.
My cat likes to play with a ball, too.

My cat wants to run.
My dog wants to run, too.

1. Прочитай и переведи.

Kate likes ice cream. She can eat a lot of ice cream. Jane likes sweets. Please take five sweets, Jane.

Ben likes apples and nuts. Bill and Lucy like cakes.

Lucy likes to skip. Does she like to swim? Does she like to roller skate? Yes, she does. She likes to swim and roller skate, too.

Ben likes to play tennis. Bill likes to ride a bike. Max likes to play the guitar and sing songs. Pete likes to fly a kite.

I want to play hockey. Mikes wants to play chess.

2. Прочитай, переведи и выучи диалоги.

ЗАПОМНИ:

very much ['verɪ 'mʌtʃ] — очень
why [waɪ] — почему

Kate: Do you like sweets?
Jane: Yes, very much.
Kate: Can you eat ten sweets?
Jane: Oh, yes!

Bill: Does Ben want to play football?
Max: No, he doesn't.
Bill: But why?
Max: He wants to roller skate.

3. Выучи новые слова. Затем прочитай и переведи текст.

rainy ['reɪnɪ]	дождливый
go for a walk ['gəu fər ə'wɔːk]	гулять
phone [fəun]	звонить

It's a rainy day. Sue isn't happy. She wants to go for a walk. She wants to play in the park. She wants to ride a bike. Jane says, 'Let's read a book!'
Sue says, 'I don't want to read. I want to go for a walk! I want to play in the park! I want to ride a bike!'
'Let's phone Phil! Let's go and see his little puppy,' says Jane. 'Oh, good!' says Sue. Sue's happy again. They phone Phil.
Phil says, 'Please come and see my little puppy. He's so nice! He likes to play with his tail. He likes to play with a ball. He likes to play with my friends.'
The girls are happy. They go and see Phil's little puppy. His puppy's soft and brown. It's so nice!

ЗАПОМНИ:

про свою собаку или кошку ты можешь сказать **he** или **she**. О чужих животных нужно сказать **it**.

4. Обведи кружком правильный ответ.

Is it a rainy day?   Yes, it is.
                     No, it isn't.

Does Sue want to go for a walk?   Yes, she does.
                                  No, she doesn't.

Does Sue want to read?	Yes, she does. No, she doesn't.
Do the girls phone Phil?	Yes, they do. No, they don't.
Do the girls go and see Phil's little puppy?	Yes, they do. No, they don't.
Does the puppy like to play with Phil's friends?	Yes, it does. No, it doesn't.
Does the puppy like to play with a ball?	Yes, it does. No, it doesn't.
Does it like to play with his tail?	Yes, it does. No, it doesn't.

5. Прочитай и выучи рифмовку.

ЗАПОМНИ:

Ted [ted] — имя мальчика
a pet [pet] — любимое животное (например, кошка, собака или птичка)

Ted has got two pets.
A cat and a white rat.
Ted likes his pets
And his pets like Ted.

Ты уже можешь сказать: **This is a cat. That's a hat.** А вот как нужно сказать то же самое, но во множественном числе: **These** [ðiːz] **are cats. Those** [ðəuz] **are hats.** (Это кошки, а вон там — шляпы.)

Прочитай и запомни:

These are pens.   Those are hens.

These are frogs.   Those are dogs.

These are cars.   Those are stars.

These are bears.    Those are hares.

These are spoons.   Those are balloons.

ЗАПОМНИ друзей **kn**, которые читаются [n].
ЗАПОМНИ звук [ɪə]. Выучи новые слова со звуками [ɪə] и [n]:

a deer [dɪə]   олень

an ear [ɪə]   ухо

a knife [naɪf] нож

a deer

an ear

a knife

6. Прочитай и переведи.

ЗАПОМНИ:

sharp [ʃɑːp] — острый

I can see a little deer. It's brown. It lives in the wood. It can run very quickly.

I can see a deer and a goat. The deer is big. The goat is small. They like to eat grass. They often want to play with children.

Children, don't play with a knife. It's very sharp. Little Kate, don't take this knife. It's very sharp.
The hare has got long ears. My dog's ears are long and soft.

7. В этих предложениях вместо некоторых слов нарисованы картинки. Назови пропущенные слова и ответь на вопросы.

What is green?   My  is green.

What is red?   My  is red.

What is black?   His  is black.

What is yellow?   My  is yellow.

What is brown?   My  is brown.

8. Прочитай, переведи и выучи рифмовки.

What is white?
I think, my kite.

What's blue?
'The sky is blue,' says little Sue.

26 My family

ВЫУЧИ НОВЫЕ СЛОВА

my dad

a family [ˈfæmɪlɪ]   семья

a granny [ˈgrænɪ]   бабушка

my mum

a mum [mʌm]   мама

a sister [ˈsɪstə]   сестра

my granddad

a brother [ˈbrʌðə]   брат

a granddad [ˈgrændæd] дедушка

1. Прочитай каждое слово по два раза.

mum mum   granddad granddad
granny granny   sister sister   brother brother

2. Прочитай и переведи.

ЗАПОМНИ:

love [lʌv] — любить

Hi! My name's Phil. I've got a big family. I've got a mum and a dad. I've got a granddad and a granny. I've got a sister and a brother. We are a happy family. I love my family. They love me.

My dad and I are good friends. We like to play football together. We often go for a walk. My little brother likes to play with his toys. He likes to play with me.

My mum and my sister are good friends, too. They like to sing songs together. They sing well.

My granddad isn't old. He's very nice. We like to make kites. We like to fly kites. My granddad wants to play hockey with me in winter.

My granny likes to make cakes. Her cakes are very nice. She often says, 'Let's make a cake, Kate.' Kate is my sister. She likes to make cakes, too.

3. Выбери и подчеркни карандашом, что любят делать в семье Фила.

My dad and I like
- to skate.
- to play football.
- to play chess.

My mum and my sister like
- to skate.
- to sing.
- to skip.

My little brother likes to read.
to write.
to play.

My granddad and I like to make cars.
to make kites.
to make ships.

My granny likes to play with dolls.
to make cakes.
to play hopscotch.

4. Прочитай слова.

[æ]	[ʌ]	[eɪ]	[ɔ]	[ŋ]
dad	mum	Kate	got	song
granddad	love	make	hockey	sing
granny	brother	cake	want	bring
family		play	hopscotch	
happy			often	

[aɪ]	[e]	[ɪ]
my	very	little
kite	let's	big
like	help	sister
nice	friends	with
fly		

5. Посмотри на картинку. Выучи новые слова. Затем прочитай и переведи текст.

a man	[mæn]	мужчина
a woman	[ˈwumən]	женщина
pretty	[ˈprɪtɪ]	хорошенький, красивый
funny	[ˈfʌnɪ]	смешной
naughty	[ˈnɔːtɪ]	озорной
kind	[kaɪnd]	добрый
clever	[ˈklevə]	умный
a parrot	[ˈpærət]	попугай
a kitten	[ˈkɪtn]	котёнок
Sam	[sæm]	имя мальчика

Look at this photo. You can see my family in it. My dad isn't a very tall man. My mum is a beautiful woman. My little sister's five. Her name's Kate. She's a pretty little girl. My brother Sam is three. He's a naughty little boy. My granddad isn't old. He's kind and clever. My granny isn't an old woman. She's very kind. You can see me, too. I'm Phil. I'm nine. You can see my pets. I've got a puppy, a parrot and a kitten. They are very funny.

6. Прочитай вопросы и подчеркни карандашом правильный ответ.

Is my dad very tall?	Yes, he is. No, he isn't.
Is my mum a beautiful woman?	Yes, she is. No, she isn't.
Is my sister a pretty little girl?	Yes, she is. No, she isn't.
Is my sister's name Kate?	Yes, it is. No, it isn't.
Is my granddad an old man?	Yes, he is. No, he isn't.
Is my brother naughty?	Yes, he is. No, he isn't.
Are my pets funny?	Yes, they are. No, they aren't.

7. Подбери слова к картинкам и обведи их кружком.

a chick, a cock, a hen, (a parrot,) a wolf, a goat

a fox, a dolphin, a zebra, an elephant, a dog

a bat, a kitten, a puppy, a pig, a bird, a fish

a fox, a puppy, a kitten, a rat, a bear, a hare

8. Соедини линией слова, которые рифмуются.

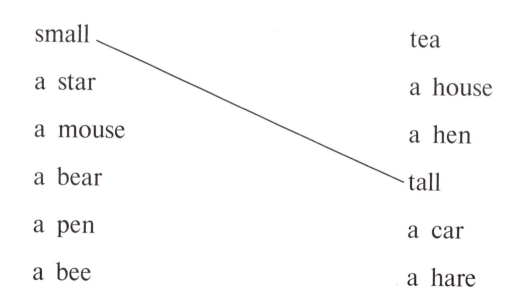

9. Прочитай и переведи.

ЗАПОМНИ:

a doctor ['dɔktə] — врач

work [wə:k] — работа

a teacher ['ti:tʃə] — учитель, учительница

watch TV ['wɔtʃ ti: 'vi:] — смотреть телевизор

win [wɪn] — выигрывать

hobby ['hɔbɪ] — увлечение

take photos — фотографировать

play the piano — играть на пианино

My dad is a doctor. He's a good doctor. He likes his work. He can play tennis very well. He likes to take photos. It's his hobby.
My mum is a teacher. She likes her work, too. She likes her pupils and her pupils like her. She can play the piano and sing. She sings very well.
My sister Kate doesn't go to school. She can read and write a little. She doesn't like computer games.
My little brother Sam is very funny. He's got a lot of toys. He likes to play with his toys. He likes to run. He can run very quickly. He's naughty. My mum often says, 'Please don't make noise, Sam. You are so naughty!'
My granny doesn't go to work. She helps my mum at home. She likes to watch TV with my granddad. My granddad likes to play chess with my dad, too. My granddad often wins. He's so clever!

10. Теперь прочитай текст ещё раз и ответь на эти вопросы.

Is Phil's dad a teacher?
Does he like his work?
Is Phil's mum a doctor?
Does she like her pupils?
Can she play the piano?
Can she sing?
Does she sing well?
Does Kate go to school?
Can she read and write?
Does Kate like computer games?
Is Sam funny and naughty?
Does he like to run?
Can he run quickly?
Does Phil's granny go to work?
Does she like to watch TV?
Does Phil's granddad like to play chess?
Does he often win?

11. Отгадай загадки.

ЗАПОМНИ:

speak [spiːk] — говорить
say [seɪ] — сказать

I'm nice and soft.
I like milk.
I can catch a grey mouse.

I'm nice and soft, too.
I'm a dog but not big.
I like to run and play with a ball.

I'm a bird. I can fly but I can't sing.
I'm very clever. I live in a cage.
I can speak. I can say, 'Hi! Bye!'

27 My living room

ВЫУЧИ НОВЫЕ СЛОВА

 a window

 a vase

 a piano

 an armchair

 a TV set

a window ['wɪndəu] — окно
a door [dɔ:] — дверь
a vase [vɑ:z] — ваза
a flower ['flauə] — цветок
a piano [pɪ'ænəu] — пианино
a carpet ['kɑ:pɪt] — ковёр
a TV set [ti:'vi: set] — телевизор
a bookcase ['bukkeɪs] — книжный шкаф
a curtain ['kə:tn] — штора
a picture ['pɪktʃə] — картина
an armchair ['ɑ:mtʃɛə] — кресло
a living room ['lɪvɪŋ rum] — гостиная
a wall [wɔ:l] — стена
the floor [flɔ:] — пол

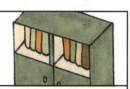 a bookcase

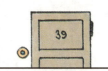 a door

 a flower

 a carpet

 a curtain

 a picture

1. Прочитай каждое слово по два раза.

window window   vase vase   piano piano
armchair armchair   TV set TV set   bookcase bookcase
curtain curtain   door door   flower flower
carpet carpet   picture picture
living room   wall floor
living room   wall floor

Если ты хочешь рассказать о том, **что**, например, находится в твоей комнате, тебе помогут слова **there is** [ðɛərˈɪz] и **there are** [ðɛərˈɑː]. Ты также сможешь рассказать о том, **кто** там находится. Со словами в единственном числе ты скажешь так:

There's a piano in the room. В комнате пианино.
(there's [ðɛəz] = there is)
There's a cat on the chair. На стуле кошка.
There's a vase on the table. На столе ваза.

Со словами во множественном числе ты скажешь так:

There are two pictures on the wall. На стене две картины.
There are four books on the sofa. На диване четыре книги.

Такие предложения называются **утвердительными**. Давай договоримся обозначать их так: **+**

Если ты поменяешь местами **there is** на **is there**, а **there are** на **are there**, ты сможешь задать вопросы. Вот так:

Is there a piano in the room?   В комнате пианино?
Is there a cat on the chair?   На стуле кошка?
Is there a vase on the table?   На столе ваза?

Are there two pictures on the wall?
На стене две картины?

Are there four books on the sofa?
На диване четыре книги?

Такие предложения называются **вопросительными**. Давай обозначим их так: **?**

Если мы с чем-то не согласны, нам поможет короткое слово **no**. Посмотри:

There's **no** piano in the room.   There's **no** cat on the chair.
В комнате нет пианино.   На стуле нет кота.

There's **no** vase on the table.
На столе нет вазы.

There are **no** pictures on the wall.
На стене нет картин.

There are **no** books on the sofa.
На диване нет книг.

Такие предложения называются **отрицательными**. Давай обозначим их так: -

Единственное число	Множественное число
+ there is	there are
? is there	are there
- there is no	there are no

2. Выбери и подчеркни карандашом правильное начало предложения. Прочитай его.

| There is / There are | a fox under the box. |

| There is / There are | a seal in the sea. |

| Is there / Are there | ten pencils in this bag? |

| Is there / Are there | a computer on the table? |

| Is there / Are there | a bird in the cage? |

| Is there |
| Are there |

two goats in the boat?

| There is |
| There are |

no rose in the vase.

3. Посмотри на картинку. Затем прочитай и переведи предложения.

There are two large windows in the living room.
There are nice curtains on the windows.
There's a big yellow sofa at the windows.
There's a brown bookcase on the right.
There are a lot of books in the bookcase.
There's a black piano on the right, too.
There are two photos on the piano.
In front of the piano there's a small chair.
There's a little green mat at the door.
There's a brown armchair next to the door.
There's a TV set on a little brown table.
In front of the TV set there's a little white table.
There's a green lamp and a green telephone on the little white table.
Next to the little white table there's a brown armchair, too.
Next to the piano there's a small brown table.
On the table there's a vase with three beautiful flowers.
There are two pictures on the wall.
There's a beautiful green carpet on the floor.

ЗАПОМНИ:

on the right [raɪt] — справа

on the left [left] — слева

next to ['nekst tə] — рядом

in front of [ɪn 'frʌnt əv] — перед

at [ət] — у

4. Закончи предложения. Для этого посмотри на картинку ещё раз. Подчеркни нужные слова. Вот так:

There's a piano | <u>on the right.</u> / on the left.

There's a bookcase | next to the piano. / in front of the piano.

There's a chair | in front of the piano. / on the piano.

There's a telephone | on the white table. / under the white table.

There are two photos | on the piano. / in front of the sofa.

There are two pictures | on the wall. / under the table.

There's a carpet | on the floor. / in the bookcase.

There's a green mat | at the door. / at the sofa.

183

5. Прочитай и скажи, что неправильно.

There's a cat on the sofa. The cat's black. The cat's fat. It can fly. It likes fish and meat.

This is a pig. It's silly. It isn't big. It likes to ride a bike. It can swim.

There's a fish in the lake. The fish is little. It's red. It can run and fly.

There's a little bird in the tree. It can sing. It likes to play the piano.

There's a wolf in the sea. It can swim. It can catch goats and hens.

There's an elephant in the lake. It likes to eat frogs. It can carry heavy logs.

6. Прочитай слова.

[ð]	[θ]	[ɑ:]	[ɔ:]	[u]	[əu]
this	thick	star	four	book	goat
that	think	car	small	wood	boat
these		park	tall	wolf	coat

7. В этой рифмовке вместо некоторых слов нарисованы картинки. Назови слова, а затем выучи всю рифмовку.

ЗАПОМНИ:

behind [bɪˈhaɪnd] — за

What's there on the chair?

There's a  on the chair.

What's there under the chair?

There's a  under the chair.

What's there behind the chair?

There's a  behind the chair.

What's there next to the chair?

There's an  next to the chair.

What's there in front of the chair?

There's a  in front of the chair.

Для того чтобы спросить, где кто-нибудь или что-нибудь находится, нам потребуется слово **Where** [wɛə]? — Где?

Посмотри внимательно и прочитай:

Where's the bear?
(Where's = where is)
Где мишка?

It's on the chair.
Он на стуле.

Where's the frog?
Где лягушонок?

It's on the log.
Он на бревне.

Where are the children?
Где дети?

They are in the wood.
Они в лесу.

Where are you?
Где ты?

I'm in the wood.
Я в лесу.

8. Прочитай и обведи кружком, что неправильно.

Where's the cat?   It's on the mat.
                             (It's in the sky.)

Where's the hare?   It's in the wood.
                             It's in the sea.

Where's the frog?   It's in the lake.
                             It's in the tree.

28 I'm reading a book now

Ты уже знаешь, как рассказать о том, что **часто** или **обычно** происходит с тобой или с твоими друзьями.

ЗАПОМНИ:

usually ['juːʒuəlɪ] — обычно

Прочитай:

I usually play snowballs in winter.
Я обычно играю в снежки зимой.

Tim reads books every day.
Тим читает книги каждый день.

They often play tennis. Они часто играют в теннис.

А теперь посмотри и прочитай, как можно рассказать о том, что происходит **сейчас** — **now** [nau]:

I am reading a book now.   Я сейчас читаю книгу.
He is riding his bike now.   Он сейчас катается на велосипеде.

They are playing snowballs now.
Они сейчас играют в снежки.

Ты видишь, что, если мы хотим рассказать о том, что происходит **сейчас**, нам помогает маленькое слово **now** и хвостик **ing** [ɪŋ], который нужно прибавить к словам, обозначающим действия.

Например:

read — reading, write — writing, fly — flying.

Кроме того, хвостику **ing** всегда помогают братья **AM**, **IS** и **ARE**.

Маленькое слово **now** не всегда играет с хвостиком **ing** и братьями **AM**, **IS** и **ARE**, но мы всегда должны о нём помнить, когда хотим рассказать о том, что происходит **сейчас**.

1. Прочитай, переведи и выучи рифмовку, чтобы всё получше запомнить.

I'm a cat. **I am sitting** on the mat.
You are a fox. **You are sitting** in the box.
It's a boy. **He is playing** with his toy.
It's a girl. **She is playing** with her doll.
We are frogs. **We are sitting** on the logs.
You are dogs. **You are playing** with the frogs.
They are hares. **They are playing** with the bears.

2. Посмотри на картинку. Затем прочитай и переведи текст.

ЗАПОМНИ:

Mummy [ˈmʌmɪ] — мамочка

sleep [sliːp] — спать

a block [blɔk] — кубик

Look at the picture. We are all sitting in the living room. Daddy and Granddad are sitting on the sofa. They are playing chess. Granddad is winning. They often play chess in the evening.

Mummy is playing the piano. She is singing a nice song, too. She likes music and usually plays the piano in the evening.

My sister is sitting on the sofa next to Daddy. She is reading a book. My sister's got a lot of books. She reads books every day. She's so clever!

My little brother is sitting on the carpet. He is playing with his blocks. He's got a lot of nice blocks.

Poll, the parrot, is sitting on the bookcase. Poll is so funny! He is looking at Daddy and Granddad.

My kitten is sleeping in the armchair.

I am standing next to the TV set. I am looking at Granny. She is watching TV. She likes to watch TV every evening.

3. Прочитай текст ещё раз. Подчеркни карандашом предложения, в которых говорится о том, что делают родственники Фила **сейчас**, одной чертой. Подчеркни предложения, в которых говорится о том, что они **часто** или **обычно** делают, двумя чертами.

4. В этом упражнении надо назвать родственников Фила. Назови их, прочитай и обведи кружком, что они сейчас делают.

 is playing chess with Granddad.
is watching TV.

1	**2**
one	two
3	**4**
three	four
5	**6**
five	six
7	**8**
seven	eight
9	**10**
nine	ten

Look at my shoe!

Who's at the door?

Give me my sticks.

Don't be late!

Write with a pen!

is singing a song.
is making a cake.

is playing tag.
is reading a book.

is playing with his blocks.
is running in the park.

is watching TV.
is playing chess.

5. Посмотри на картинки. Выучи рифмовки.

ЗАПОМНИ:

finger [ˈfɪŋɡə] — палец на руке

toe [təu] — палец на ноге

shoe [ʃuː] — ботинок

He's got ten fingers.
He's got ten toes.
He's got two ears, two eyes
And one little nose.